STUDIES IN
ANTHROPOLOGICAL METHOD

General Editors

GEORGE AND LOUISE SPINDLER
Stanford University

D1520405

FIELD METHODS
IN THE STUDY OF CULTURE

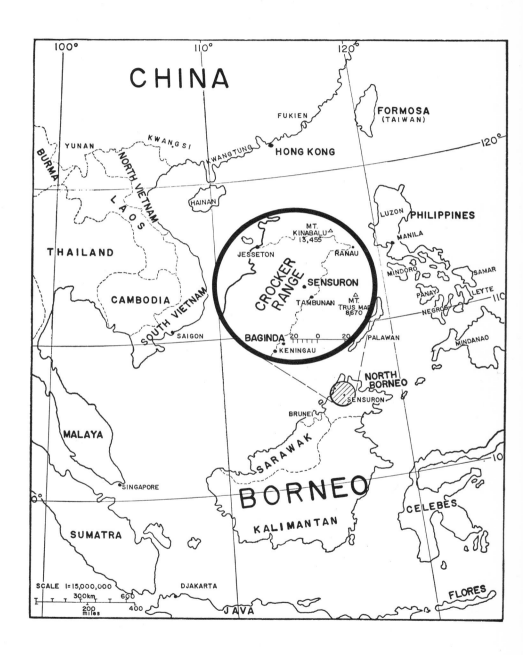

FIELD METHODS
IN THE STUDY
OF CULTURE

THOMAS RHYS WILLIAMS
The Ohio State University

HOLT, RINEHART AND WINSTON
New York Chicago San Francisco Atlanta
Dallas Montreal Toronto London

Copyright © 1967 by Holt, Rinehart and Winston, Inc.
All rights reserved
Library of Congress Catalog Card Number: 66–18798
Printed in the United States of America
ISBN: 0-03-053095-4

89   059   98

FOREWORD

ABOUT THE SERIES

Anthropology has been, since the turn of the century, a significant influence shaping Western thought. It has brought into proper perspective the position of our culture as one of many and has challenged universalistic and absolutistic assumptions and beliefs about the proper condition of man. Anthropology has been able to make this contribution mainly through its descriptive analyses of non-Western ways of life. Only in the last decades of its comparatively short existence as a science have anthropologists developed systematic theories about human behavior in its transcultural dimensions, and only very recently have anthropological techniques of data collection and analysis become explicit and in some instances replicable.

Teachers of anthropology have been handicapped by the lack of clear, authoritative statements of how anthropologists collect and analyze relevant data. The results of fieldwork are available in the ethnographies and they can be used to demonstrate cultural diversity and integration, social control, religious behavior, marriage customs, and the like, but clear, systematic statements about how the facts are gathered and interpreted are rare in the literature readily available to students. Without this information the alert reader of anthropological literature is left uninformed about the process of our science, knowing only of the results. This is an unsatisfying state of affairs for both the student and the instructor.

This series is designed to help solve this problem. Each study in the series focuses upon manageable dimensions of modern anthropological methodology. Each one demonstrates significant aspects of the processes of gathering, ordering, and interpreting data. Some are highly selected dimensions of methodology. Others are concerned with the whole range of experience involved in studying a total society. These studies are written by professional anthropologists who have done fieldwork and have made significant contributions to the science of man and his works. In them the authors explain how they go about this work, and to what end. We think they will be helpful to students who want to know what processes of inquiry and ordering stand behind the formal, published results of anthropology.

ABOUT THE AUTHOR

Thomas Rhys Williams is a professor and chairman of the department of anthropology at Ohio State University. He holds a master of arts degree from the University of Arizona and a doctoral degree from Syracuse University. He has engaged in field research among the Papago of Arizona and the native peoples of Borneo. His interests in field research include enculturation, social structure, nonverbal communication, and cultural structuring of perceptions, including touch, color, and sight. He has published several professional articles and a case study of the Dusun of North Borneo, and is completing a text on enculturation in the communities he worked in there.

He is a fellow of the American Anthropological Association, a member of the Society of Sigma Xi, and other professional associations.

ABOUT THE BOOK

This study by Thomas Rhys Williams covers a wide range of the methods used by anthropologists in the study of culture. His research experience in Dusun communities is utilized for illustration. The reader will find information on the problems encountered in selecting a community for study, coping with the physical and social hazards of isolation from one's own kind in a strange environment, recording observations, and maintaining roles and status that permit close and friendly contact but at the same time preserve a basic scientific orientation. Dr. Williams takes us from the early planning stages of a research project to the termination of the study in the field. The anthropologist emerges from these pages as a human being with respect for the qualities of his informants. There are, of course, some technical aspects of data collection and analysis that are touched upon only briefly.

No short study of methods in cultural anthropology can cover the many and complex details of method and technique. The virtue of Dr. Williams' presentation is that the field experience of the anthropologist is seen whole and as a human experience. Though no two anthropologists have exactly the same experiences in the field, most will recognize their own on the pages to follow.

GEORGE AND LOUISE SPINDLER
General Editors
Stanford, 1967

CONTENTS

FIELD METHODS
IN THE STUDY OF CULTURE

Introduction

CULTURAL ANTHROPOLOGISTS tend to concentrate their research efforts on small, isolated societies.[1] This book is about some of the special research problems anthropologists encounter in these societies.

The professional training of the cultural anthropologist includes courses in methods and usually requires that a year or more be spent in residence in a community gathering data for a thesis for the doctorate of philosophy degree.[2] It is in graduate courses and from the experience of living in a society other than his own that the anthropology student usually comes to learn the ways of recognizing and dealing with the special problems of the study of culture. There is also a substantial body of knowledge concerning these research problems that is acquired from conversations between graduate professors and students, and between students sharing the experiences of field study. Such training enables anthropologists to read technical reports without a lengthy preface concerning the methods of study used. Conversely, a reader without professional anthropological training finds it difficult to evaluate an ethnographic account because of lack of knowledge of the procedures that have been used in recording data. This difficulty can be dealt with, at least partially, through reading professional literature on field methods. Such accounts, however, are often based on conventional under-

---

[1] Such study is less difficult than it would be in a society numbering millions of persons; it is easier to determine the facts of sharing and the varieties of custom among a small group than in a large population. Cultural anthropologists feel it a special responsibility of their discipline to make detailed records of all the possible variations of human custom. Special attention is being given to those societies isolated from contact with the modern world. Studies of culture are also being conducted in modern, urbanized Western society, with the modification of field methods discussed here and in professional anthropological literature. See, for instance, Gallaher (1961).

[2] Anthropology has several areas of specialized study. The student of culture is called a *cultural* or *social anthropologist,* and may be referred to as an *ethnographer* when living in a society for the purpose of describing its culture.

1

standings of field research shared by anthropologists as the consequence of professional training and do not communicate effectively to those who have not had this training.

This study illustrates some of the ways cultural anthropologists conduct research. Examples are given in the text from my work among the Dusun of North Borneo. It is not proposed that my particular field experiences among the Dusun are representative of those of every cultural anthropologist. Some of the methods I have used can be applied in a study of culture in any society, and where the specific methods used are not transferable, parallels to them will be discussed.

The Dusun comprise a population of some 145,650 persons concentrated in the mountain jungle highlands of North Borneo.[3] Descriptions of some forms of Dusun custom by colonial government officers and travelers are to be found in the works of Rutter (1929) and Evans (1922, 1953). From August 1959 to August 1960 my wife and I resided in Sensuron, a Dusun community of 947 persons in the Tambunan district of the North Borneo Interior Residency.[4] From September 1962, through August 1963, with our thirteen-month-old son, we resided in Baginda, a Dusun community of 751 persons in the Keningau district of the Interior Residency. Baginda village is located some 70 miles south of Sensuron. I have reported on Dusun culture in a case study in cultural anthropology and in a variety of professional publications (1960, 1961a, 1961b, 1962a, 1962b, 1962c, 1963a, 1963b, 1965, 1966). During our residence in the two Dusun communities an effort was made to record the behavior of adults. We also were studying the techniques used by adults to transmit culture to children as they mature in these Dusun communities. Since our own field experience provides the major source for illustration of general principles for the study of culture put forward in this book, the reader may profit by familiarizing himself with the Dusun through the references cited and particularly through reading the case study *The Dusun: A North Borneo Society* (1965).

The discussion that follows is organized about the events which most often occur in the study of culture: the making of preparations for research; the initial period of study—first contacts and setting up of residence; and the problems of obtaining, recording, and dealing with data. Attention is then given briefly to the questions of the kinds of statuses and roles open to the anthropologist as he conducts research in a native group and to the problems of termination of research. Finally, some comment is given regarding topics implicit in and related to methods for the study of culture.

---

[3] *North Borneo, Report on the Census of Population Taken on 10 August, 1960.* Kuching, Sarawak: Government Printer, 1962.
[4] The term "native" is occasionally used in this discussion. Wherever it occurs, it carries only the meaning of "people living in an area or country." The term is not derogatory and is not intended to demean or detract from any group to which it is applied. There is no meaning here of intellectual, cultural, social, economic, political, or personal inferiority of any group to which the term is applied.

My wife Peggy and my son Rhys lived under difficult conditions and shared in learning with me about the nature of culture. I could not have accomplished my research and writing without their understanding. My son Ian has also helped me learn about culture. We owe a debt of gratitude to our Dusun friends. It is their tolerance, wisdom, good humor, and kindness to strangers which has made our work possible. Many persons assisted in our studies. We especially want to thank John and Brenda Fryer of the Colonial North Borneo Lands and Survey Department; *O.K.K.* G. S. Sundang, now Deputy Chief Minister, and Minister for Local Government, Sabah, Malaysia; and our good friend and very capable interpreter, Anthony Gibon, now Sabah State Senator from Tambunan.[5] And we owe much to Stephen Awong, our Baginda friend, assistant, and interpreter. My work in North Borneo was supported by research grants from the National Science Foundation (G–5018; G–22110) and the Joint Committee on Asian Studies, American Council of Learned Societies—Social Science Research Council (1959, 1962), and conducted with assistance from Eli Lilly Company and Abbott Laboratories. I am solely responsible for the conclusions and comments in this work. I would like to dedicate this work to all the fieldworkers whose years in isolated places have made it possible to systematically discuss field methods in the study of culture.

---

[5] In September 1963 the colony of North Borneo became the state of Sabah, in Malaysia. The designation "North Borneo" has been retained in this text only because the research discussed here was conducted prior to the independence of the area as a part of Malaysia.

1

Choosing a Location

THE FACTORS that determine which society to study vary between anthropologists. The choice of an anthropologist completing his doctoral degree to live and study in a geographic region and with a particular people often depends upon the research interests and experiences of the professors who guide his graduate training.[1] And it may also be a reflection of the fact that the university at which a degree is sought is sponsoring special or intensive studies of a particular culture region, such as Meso-America or Mainland Southeast Asia.[2] For the professional anthropologist and, to a certain extent, for the doctoral student in anthropology, the choice of a particular group for study often derives from an interest in the testing of particular research hypotheses in a cultural setting not yet known through reports based on long-term residence by a trained scholar.

---

[1] At the Fourth International Congress of Anthropological and Ethnological Sciences in Vienna, in 1952, a special session was devoted to a symposium concerning the most urgent tasks of research in anthropology. This resulted in an "International Committee on Urgent Anthropological and Ethnological Research" being appointed in 1956 from the International Union of Anthropological and Ethnological Sciences with support from the Fifth International Congress of Anthropological and Ethnological Sciences in 1956. At the general session of UNESCO in New Delhi, in 1956, a resolution was adopted to sponsor the work of the Committee. Publications of the Committee provide details of location and information concerning tribes or societies apparently close to being absorbed into a larger society or in the process of profound cultural change. An anthropologist can choose to study such a group if he is interested. See Heine-Geldern (1958) for an example of committee reports. Since 1956 many of these societies have disintegrated.

[2] The phrase "culture region" refers to the fact that within certain geographic regions of the world there are clusters of particular traits of custom.

Bibliographic Preparation

While reviewing studies of the process of cultural transmission in the anthropological literature, I found that there appeared to have been no systematic research on the topic in Borneo. I began a systematic reading of the published information on Borneo and its native peoples. The reading lasted a year. In that year I also queried colleagues in anthropology and other disciplines about their knowledge of Borneo. I concluded that little was known and that no systematic studies of cultural transmission had been undertaken on the island. I then proceeded to draft a research proposal for a field study among the Dusun of northern Borneo.

Writing a Research Proposal

The writing of a research proposal involves the setting forth, in specific detail, and with some exactness, the answers to the following questions: (1) What is it you propose to do? (2) How do you propose to accomplish the research? (3) What research of this type has been undertaken before, particularly among the group to be studied? (4) What is the estimated amount of funds needed to support the research? (5) What period of time is to be devoted to the research? The form of research proposals can vary widely in inclusion of detail and with individual writing styles, but in most instances should provide direct answers to these questions. Such a statement is necessary since it provides a useful guide for study and because the solicitation of funds for support of research usually requires such statements. It is a sound rule to write and use a research statement, even if you support your own studies.

Support for fieldwork is provided by a number of private foundations, governmental agencies, and through money available to graduate anthropology departments from local university scholarship and research grant funds. The graduate student setting out to complete his training often receives aid in his work through funds available to his graduate department. He may, however, formulate a research proposal and submit it, in competition with other graduate students, for consideration for a research grant. At present the National Science Foundation, the Public Health Service, and the Ford Foundation, with other smaller research foundations, provide modest amounts of money to assist in the training of anthropologists. These same foundations also make awards to qualified scholars submitting proposals for research. The proposals of anthropologists are judged by panels of senior anthropological scholars and administrative officers of the foundations for their merits in terms of advancing anthropological knowledge. Awards of funds for support of anthropological study provide some indication of the likelihood that the research proposal makes theoretical and methodological sense, and may even lead to new knowledge, if the work proposed is completed.

When I had finished writing a proposal for research on the culture of the Dusun, I submitted it to several senior colleagues specializing in studies of cultural transmission and with special interests in the peoples and cultures of Southeast Asia. Their criticism enabled me to redraft the statement to make it more direct in expression and concise in form. I also contacted a colleague who had worked in North Borneo. A fieldworker should always contact anthropologists who have worked in the area of the proposed research to ask them for advice on the study and to offer one's help in seeking data they may specially need. Such courtesy may result in access to valuable unpublished material, letters of introduction, loans of out-of-print books or old census lists, old photographs, and other items which can be of invaluable help in the field. With the proposal in a revised form I proceeded to the formulation of a budget to support the first period of study among the Dusun.

Making a Budget

I drew up a list of all costs we could anticipate that would occur during our study. I put the budget in three parts. First, I estimated costs of external travel, that is, travel from my home to the location of research in Borneo, including fares for airplane or ship, taxi fares, hotels, meals, train or bus fares, tips, and services. Then I estimated the costs of equipment and supplies for fifteen months' research. These costs included purchase of cameras, films, tape recorder, tapes, paper, pencils, paper clips, filing boxes, the renting or building and furnishing of a native style house in a Dusun village, and the costs of research supplies. I tried to estimate the costs of travel in Borneo in order to make comparisons between forms of local custom. In this estimate I included air, train, bus, and taxi fares, hotels, meals, and services. I then added these three sets of figures and put them together as the first of two budget proposals. The first estimate I considered to be the amount I needed to do an adequate job of research. I made a second set of budget figures, comparable in detail to the first, but lower than my first estimates. These budget figures I considered as those which would enable us to get to Borneo, live in a Dusun community, and return home, without any travel for comparative purposes and little use of recording devices such as cameras, tapes, and so on. I put these two budget proposals in my research statement to give the foundations a choice of budgets, with a difference of about 20 percent between the highest and lowest figures. I did not include a request for salary; although such an item is usual for budget proposals now, in the 1950s funds for research were so much more restricted that inclusion of such an item would often eliminate a proposal from consideration by a foundation.

I found on returning after the first period of study among the Dusun that I had underestimated our budget. My highest budget estimate was the one finally granted me in the basic anthropology research grant program of the National Science Foundation. However, I had neglected to include a variety of minor costs, such as money transfer, currency exchange, service charges on banking accounts, use of the telephone, postage for correspondence related to the study, driver's licenses, gun licenses, permits and taxes of a variety of kinds levied by the local governments (such as a fee for boarding an airplane charged in Hongkong and Singapore). The air and ship fares were also raised by some 10 percent in the year of our study, thereby adding to the total expense of travel. I had not estimated accurately the costs of repairs to cameras and tape recorders, the purchase of medical supplies locally, the necessary return of entertainment provided by local government officials and business leaders, the purchase or rental of boats for river transport, the costs of having rafts built when unable to cross flooded streams; and I neglected to anticipate fully the expenses of entertainment of Dusun while in residence, including celebrations (described in Chapter 2) I found necessary to host for the community.

I had failed to anticipate the costs that I would have to pay to wait for several weeks in entering and leaving a village, while making arrangements for supplies, travel, and mail. It is probably wise to plan any field study in an unfamiliar society to include at least a month of waiting to make and, later, terminate arrangements for living in a community. I did not request funds for processing data or secretarial assistance in writing reports. These costs can add greatly to the expenses of fieldwork.

The most important point about making a budget is that there will be many unanticipated costs in a field study, which must be met, if the work is to be carried on with any meaning. Some of these extra costs probably can be anticipated; but in an area of the world with poor medical services, inadequate transportation, and dangerous living conditions, any one of a number of events, from shipwreck to rebellion, can throw a budget for research out of balance and be very inadequate. It would be a sound procedure to always try to include a budget item for field emergencies and leave it unchanged in any budget estimate.

Preparations for Study

In the six months after my research proposal and budgets had been submitted for consideration by the National Science Foundation, I proceeded to make preparations for study in Borneo. I sent six copies of my research proposal to the British Ambassador in Washington, D.C., to the British Colonial Office in London, and to the Chief Secretary of the Colony of North Borneo, and requested, in each case, review, comment on, and permission to undertake the research. At the same time I made necessary preparations to have valid passports for travel and to insure that my physical condition and my wife's were such that we could be isolated from medical care for long periods of time.

I also made lists of equipment that I would have to send by sea from the United States. Since we could find little contemporary published information on Borneo living conditions, I was forced to guess at the availability of much of the equipment and supplies I felt we would need in our study. My principal sources of information on current living conditions in the (then) British territories came from a few comments by colleagues, from letters from a missionary in Sarawak, from lists of prices and goods sent by a merchant in Jesselton, the capital of North Borneo, and from a bulletin written for wives of colonial officers being assigned to North Borneo. The bulletin was helpful to some extent, but failed to meet our field needs as it was more concerned with suggestions for bringing proper table settings and formal wear for use at garden parties and receptions.

We finally concentrated on shipping a stock of medical supplies, reference materials I felt vital to the study, paper and tape recording supplies, and reading materials. In a university bookstore we purchased many copies of the required paperback readings in literature courses, and also selected a large stock of paperback novels from the general collection. Anyone who plans to isolate himself for a year or more in a native community would be well advised to follow a similar plan for some change of pace. Fieldwork usually involves a very long day, and provision must be made for relaxation. A small battery-operated record player and records, or use of musical tapes with field recording equipment could help also. Books read in the field tend to have a greater impact than when read at home, since your awareness of yourself and of life experiences will be enhanced and sharpened in fieldwork. For this reason literature which has merited critical acclaim is useful. All books read should be noted in the diary notes kept of daily observations. There are important theoretical points in the professional literature you read that may be brought out more distinctly in your research, and there may be overlapping theories in different texts which contribute to your understanding of data being recorded. Daily notes on your reading help you return to the point of first concern with an idea.

It is helpful to have all the inoculations obtainable, beyond those required for travel by most governments. It would be wise not to wait until the weeks just before leaving to have innoculations. Mistakes in vital preparations can result from reactions to overlapping innoculations. And it is useful to be aware of the kinds of disease problems to be faced in the conditions under which the study will be conducted and to try to learn in detail proper preventative procedures for maintaining health over a long period in a situation which generally is unhealthy. Before leaving we sought advice from specialists in communicable and tropical disease regarding diseases we knew we should probably encounter in Borneo. We found this information most useful in making decisions while in the field.

Some Travel Procedures

It is probably well to insure that when you travel to the field you carry a duplicate copy of birth certificates, health cards and multiple copies of the research proposal. We have experienced the mislaying of our passports and health certificates by customs and health officials. A duplicate copy of a health card and a birth certificate can often serve to allow you to continue to travel to your destination. Copies of the research proposal are useful in explaining to officials the kind of work you intend to do. A "To whom it may concern" letter from the head of your academic institution and from professors to colleagues in that area will also be useful in explaining your research and serve as a personal introduction.[3] While such questions are rarely asked on heavily traveled main routes, most foreigners in out-of-the-way areas will be questioned about their visit or travel, since the official visa stamp usually means little a long distance from a national capital. The duplicate research proposal will be especially helpful if you have purchased a variety of recording equipment, such as a large quantity of film or cameras or a tape recorder, which you are carrying with you because of the difficulties of shipping delicate items. The presence of such equipment is likely to result in some pointed questions, for which the research proposal can at least provide a point from which to start talking. You should be aware that political conditions are very complex at present; a place that was accessible three months before can be closed to you on arrival. You will need all the detailed advice you can gather before leaving; even then, you may arrive to find the political situation has changed in a matter of days.

If you can do so without unduly delaying travel or causing extra expense, it may be very helpful to spend time in the cities enroute to the field study, visiting persons with some special knowledge of the people or the land, and it is always helpful to make contacts at the nearest university or college for exchanges of ideas and data, and perhaps to arrange for help in identification of plant or animal specimens which are related to the study. If there is a museum in the area of your research, it usually is advisable to look through the collections and talk with curators concerning your study. This information and contact can be most useful, since there may be material available to you at this point which you can find nowhere else.

Arriving at the Location of Study

The few days following arrival at the general location of proposed research are usually very important to the general conduct of the study. Yet,

---

[3] Letters of introduction are also a matter of simple courtesy. An anthropologist contacts colleagues and officials in the area of his research as a matter of politeness and not because of a desire to use others for his own ends.

they tend to be among the more difficult for the inexperienced fieldworker, because of the physical acclimation needed to the area, with its sometimes quite drastic changes in diet and climate, and due often to the very different procedures in such simple matters as making a telephone call, seeking directions, or finding a place to eat. It is usually vital that official visits be made immediately upon representatives of the local government. Such visits may involve procedures that are not described in any literature available to the fieldworker; thus, in arriving in a Borneo territory controlled by the British, it was considered "good form" to stop enroute to the hotel to sign our name and purpose of visit in a large volume kept in the sentry box at the foot of the drive to the colonial governor's residence. It was also necessary to repeat the action at the office of the chief secretary to the governor. Failure to be aware of and observe such local custom can result in less than enthusiastic support from local officials. We learned from both officials that each took time to read these books and that both held very strong and negative opinions of the manners and character of persons failing to observe the custom of "signing the book." We had the good fortune to be warned of these feelings of the top government officials by comments made by a local merchant whom we met enroute to North Borneo.

To make the course of needed official cooperation easier than might otherwise be the case, it also will help to learn of local ethnocentrism and local personalities. A colonial official with a dislike of Americans, a native department head in a newly free country, or a harrassed bureaucrat can put blocks in the path of a study because of sensibilities offended by a supposed lack of "manners" by a visitor unaware of local custom. If you are suffering from the changes in diet and climate, as we were on our arrival in North Borneo, and have acquired one of the local varieties of colds and intestinal infections, you may find your initial contacts to be a perspiration-filled, stomach-aching effort to explain simply a complex, carefully prepared and planned research effort to sometimes hostile, sometimes bored officials.

It is usually appropriate to solicit the aid of local government officials in choosing the exact location for study. A request for assistance and advice may provide an opportunity to correct any breaches of manners committed in the first visits. Local officials can set up personal contacts that may considerably lessen problems of supply, medical assistance, and protection in case of need. Our research was helped considerably through the personal aid of several junior officials in cutting "red tape" for us. It is useful to anticipate that there will be no necessary relationship between the length of service of an official and his knowledge of particular areas of the country. An official may or may not have traveled in the area of proposed study (not all Americans have been to northern Wyoming) and he may be very prejudiced about the people chosen for study because of long-standing local cultural differences. We found the official responsible for native affairs, in forty years' service in the country, had not been into the area we planned to live in during our study.

The selection of a merchant to supply equipment is in most ways as sensitive a matter as first visits to local government officials. A great deal of local pride, antagonism, and long-standing argument may come to focus on the fieldworker if he chooses a merchant from one ethnic group over another. Usually, a local merchant can give helpful advice on the general types of equipment best fitted for residence in a native community and the best kinds of presents to be given to informants and friends. Guesses concerning presents that might please people can be expensive and even dangerous; for example, choices of the wrong color beads where the color is feared or disliked can cause difficulties in a community.

With a variety of kinds of advice in hand, it is still useful, before proceeding, to make a tour of the general region of the study. The possibilities for such a tour will be limited by the funds and time available, but the benefits are great. Our initial travel to many areas of North Borneo by plane, boat, and road gave us perspective on the official advice we had been given and some more specific ideas of our needs. We gained a fairly accurate idea of the distribution and style of life of people, the routes of transport of supplies, the variations in climate and topography, and came to know generally the kinds of conditions with which we would have to cope in a native village. And the time spent away from the government center allowed us to form impressions of our responses to our experiences.

With some knowledge of the country, local conditions, and personalities, and with equipment ordered in a general form, it is still necessary to make a choice for the precise location of the research. This choice may be forced by a local political official's decision to restrict the fieldworker to the study of a certain area. Many governments do not wish to have outsiders become aware of the lack of health, school, and transport facilities in some of the more remote regions of their countries since this fact is at variance with their public statements. And many newly free nations are sensitive to the fact that there are "native" peoples in their countries and would hide the fact through prohibitions of travel into those areas. In some countries a state of local insurrection, revivalistic movements (such as the "cargo cult"), tax rebellions, declining or presumably declining populations, or any of a wide variety of social, economic, or political conditions may result in denial of access to particular areas.[4]

If the choice of location is a relatively free one, then the factors to be dealt with must involve a variety of questions that begin with the research proposal and continue through personal health and safety. It should be determined if the region chosen has a high density population of the group you would study, whether or not culture changes are drastically affecting the region, the ease or difficulty of travel into and out of the area, the possible medical and personal safety problems, the availability in the area of persons to serve as interpreters, and the general local reputation of

---

[4] On this point see Hortense Powdermaker *Stranger and Friend* (1966: 55) in which she describes how she was forbidden to go to *Mafulu* in New Guinea.

the region as "representative" of the native culture. These questions can only be answered with reference to the adequacy of your local information, your initial travel in the country, and your evaluation of the possibilities of doing the type of research proposed.[5] There are students of anthropology who want to go to only the supposedly "untouched" natives of a culture region. The desire to excel other anthropologists—to be "first"—is properly a part of the motivation that leads a fieldworker to studies of remote peoples. But most persons wanting to go to the "untouched" natives have no real idea of the problems of research under such conditions. A substantial investment of time and effort goes into the training of the anthropologist. His welfare is important to his colleagues. A sick anthropologist is not a working anthropologist. The picture of the research specialist trudging off into the jungle with little more than a change of socks, a toothbrush, and notebook is appealing over a "coke" and cheeseburger in a campus snack shop. There is a difference, however, between this idealized picture and being very lost, hungry, wet, sore, exhausted, and bleeding from leeches. Anthropologists do travel to and live with very isolated peoples in the most remote parts of the world. They are usually experienced professionals, fully aware of the risks they take and prepared to cope with most emergencies. It has been said: "The fewer the adventures, the better the fieldwork."

---

[5] There are a variety of other problems in fieldwork which have not been mentioned, but which are important to its conduct. Some of these are: (1) carrying spare glasses and prescriptions and copies of personal medication prescriptions; (2) clothes for formal events at government functions, and ways of protecting them in storage; (3) knowledge of local drinking customs, style, precedence, toasts; (4) awareness of the ways in which compulsory hospitality by officials can be repaid; (5) proper ways of dealing with one's own and other person's servants, manners of dressing servants, tips, means of relaying messages by servants; (6) the details of local civil service ranks; (7) local emoluments for residents and visitors: some hospital care may be free, while all dental care may be charged to you; (8) liability for foreign sales and income taxes—whether your research funds in the country are subject to income tax charges; (9) customs regulations and duties on importing scientific equipment and personal luggage; (10) registration of foreign-made equipment with U.S. customs to avoid payment of duties on return; (11) insurance costs for coverage on all cameras, tape recorders, typewriters, and other equipment, and, (12) income tax liabilities on grant funds to federal and state governments: no grant funds are "tax free." You may deduct research and travel expenses to certain limits, but you must keep very detailed records of expenses and report your income in detail.

2

Entering a Native Community

THE LOCAL GOVERNMENT OFFICIALS of a region chosen for study are important to the conduct of research. They can provide assistance in case of need, valuable advice on local cultural variations, many personal contacts, and make available records and documents related to the study. It is very useful to take the time to explain to all senior local government officials the nature of your research and the specific ways you propose to proceed. In this way rapport can be gained with persons who are likely to be officially charged with responsibility for your safety and conduct.[1] In the course of such discussions it may be possible to acquire information concerning the local political structure. Awareness of this structure and its functioning may aid in avoiding future problems.

Once initial contacts have been established, it is helpful to ask the senior local government officer to introduce you to the officials working under his direction. In many countries native societies are administered by the central government through officials appointed from the group. Although titles and powers vary considerably, the "native chief" usually transmits orders from the central government to the local communities and can be the means for expression of native political concerns with the larger society. Native officials can assist in choosing specific village locations for study, and may serve as intermediaries in first contacts. Before accepting assistance, it would be useful to try to learn something of their place in local political affairs. Friendship with a native official can sometimes aid greatly in establishing contacts in a village or it can make a study very difficult. Talks with local merchants, traders and missionaries and natives will usually provide information on the role of a particular native official in local politics.

---

[1] It is a considerable responsibility for a local official to allow an anthropologist to travel and live in remote and unstable areas, especially if a woman and children are involved. For a poignant account of the experiences of the wife of an anthropologist see Patricia Hitchcock, "Our Ulleri Child," *Redbook,* 127:20–26, August 1966.

My first visit to Sensuron was made in the company of the district officer and one of the "native chiefs" of the area. We had a cool reception. I learned later from local merchants that there had been disagreements in the past between the Sensuron head man and the native chief. In talking with a group of Dusun men from other villages as they drank rice wine at a weekly market, I learned my reception in Sensuron was even more reserved than I had suspected because I had come to the community with the local district officer.

The choice of a specific native community for residence will depend upon the type of research to be conducted, factors of physical accessibility, population size and composition, local hostility to outsiders, village health conditions, space available for a house site, village position with reference to main roads or trails, and local potential for study of the general culture. Although most current studies of a culture are based on long-term residence in one community, it is not unusual for an anthropologist with a special research problem to spend varying periods in several villages in a region. The most direct way to determine the suitability of a community is to travel in the area in company with a well-known and respected native official, meeting village leaders and talking about the study.

Depending on the information you gather from such visits, it should be possible to select several communities for possible residence. It would be useful to return again to each of these to gather more information about the local culture and to see about arrangements for living in the community. A second visit made without the company of local officials may eliminate making a choice of a residence which could limit, or delay, your study. We finally chose Sensuron for our first residence because it was the largest native community in North Borneo, it appeared to be culturally conservative in the Dusun tradition, it was generally isolated from contact with the larger North Borneo society, and it was reported to be a point from which the nearby Tambunan area had been settled.

When a final choice of residence is made, arrangements can be completed for living in the community. Sometimes living quarters can be obtained through seeking a native family to take you as a part of the household. Generally, it is necessary to arrange the details of building, purchase, or rental of a house. Since this may involve exchange of money or goods, and the work time of villagers, it may take some time to complete living arrangements. Temporary quarters of some type can usually be obtained while a house is being prepared. In Sensuron we rented the village headman's house for about five dollars a month. The house was already a focal point of daily village routines and centrally located. The headman moved next door into another house. We established residence with little delay. In Baginda we had a house built in the village and had to wait a time before moving in. Meanwhile we lived at a government "rest house" some 10 miles away and drove to the village every day.

In the time before intensive research begins, general details of housekeeping should be completed. An anthropologist alone in the field will find a substantial amount of his time devoted to the tasks of staying fed, clean, and healthy. This investment of time can be reduced if assistants from the community are employed to aid in domestic tasks. Whether one or several persons are hired depends on individual budgets and needs. A married fieldworker will usually find that his wife will need help in such activities as gathering firewood, washing clothes, carrying water, and obtaining local foods. And it may be that the local community would feel offended if such activities were done by a European female. Our Dusun friends made it quite clear that they did not approve of my wife doing such tasks because she was supposed to "rest" for the medical care she gave at the daily clinics. Selection of household assistants should be done with care and, if possible, in accord with local beliefs. In some culture areas it is not possible for an unmarried anthropologist to regularly employ an unmarried household assistant of the opposite sex, while in others it is difficult to avoid the matchmaking intents or definitions of hospitality in the native community. Household assistants can serve as key informants (see Chapter 3), often are an important source of social contacts in the community, and provide opportunity for practice in use of the language.

When arrangements for living are being made, a plan can be devised for maintaining personal health, taking into account local conditions. Household assistants should be examined for communicable diseases if a medical officer is available in the area. Care should be used in obtaining drinking water; rivers and springs near isolated communities are often infected. Even if rain is collected from gutters on a house roof, the precautions of boiling all water, as well as properly filtering and storing it, should be used regularly. It is important that you be aware of personal hygiene. Small cuts can become rapidly infected. Local medical officers can give you a great deal of information on diseases to be found in the area. If you have not had simple first aid training, it would be well to learn elementary procedures for treatment of burns, fractures, wounds, and so on. It is very likely that in most isolated communities people will turn to you for emergency first aid. If it can be arranged before going into the field, it might be useful to spend some time in the emergency room of a large city hospital learning to differentiate between a genuine emergency and a need for simple first aid, and in getting accustomed to the sights, sounds, and smells of accidents. It is very helpful to have witnessed a childbirth or to study a film of birth, and to have some experience at scenes of death from an accident in an emergency room. These experiences can prepare you for the "life shock" to be encountered in a remote society as you face the processes of life, birth and death, mutilation, ulcerated sores, worms being vomited through the nostrils, and so on. These experiences cannot prepare you for the "culture shock" which results from living closely with people whose cultural categorizations of experience will be totally alien in many ways. Culture shock should not be confused with life shock. Life shock can be reduced greatly with some study and preparation before fieldwork. Culture shock is an experience that can only be dealt with in the field on the basis of the situation and your perceptions of your own culture and the local culture. In our Dusun field-work we were asked for first aid in childbirth, burns, amputations, major cuts from fights, and fractures; for help in treating epidemic diseases; and to alleviate pain from terminal cancers. My wife held clinics twice daily and we made it known we would come to give aid in the village. Her train-ing as a registered nurse and teacher of nursing and my previous field experience proved of great help in our work since it did prepare us for "life shock."

The First Month of Study

The first days of residence in a native community are vital to your research. In this time you will be communicating the intent of your work and self. Whatever explanation you use for your work, it is important that it be accurate, honest, and open. In the first period of research you will also be making observations which may be crucial to subsequent analyses of cultural data. The initial days of residence are likely to be filled with quite varied and conflicting impressions of the ways of the people and the physi-cal setting of the community. These initial impressions should be recorded in detail to allow a subsequent return to them. Early in the first night we were in Sensuron, we heard chanting in the headman's house. I went next door, sat, listened, and watched as five adolescents squatted about the fire pit singing a chant in Dusun. I learned these five young adults were the recent converts to Christianity in the village. Their chant turned out to be a part of the rosary. The event was staged by the headman, a "pagan" to help us "feel at home so far from our friends." The notes of this first night helped to place later notes of Dusun beliefs concerning social relations between nonrelated persons in their proper context.

It will be necessary to make known the purposes and procedures of your study. This can be done by arranging a celebration for the entire com-munity.[2] At the celebration, which should be held sometime during the first weeks of residence, it may be possible to describe your work and be seen by most members of the community. Without a community celebration it may take months to establish social relationships with many persons vital to your study. This aim can also be met in a limited manner through holding a celebration for a group of related households and inviting village leaders to participate. It probably is not wise to make promises at these celebrations. You should be discreet concerning any information you give about yourself and your relatives until you are sure of the meaning of such comment in local life. Do not promise photographs unless you can provide them to all.

---

[2] It will be difficult in some cultures to arrange a celebration until the local forms of community leisure activity are understood. It may be several months in a culture before explanations can be given concerning your research.

In Sensuron we held celebrations for the neighborhood and later for the entire village. The day of the neighborhood party was spent in preparation of food and drink for the some sixty persons, including the political leaders of the area who were invited to attend. Our house was filled with Dusun women making various foods and preparing bamboo cups for drinking. My wife was doing well with a strange language and the food preparation until the headman came into the kitchen area carrying the front half of a large pig with blood dripping down onto the floor. He was followed by three men lugging a hind quarter of a large water buffalo and a skewer of guts. When the buffalo was laid alongside the pig half, the men stepped back to look at my wife's cooking skills. Her response was a calm comment that she did not know how to butcher for cooking; with a grin, the headman admitted it was all a joke since that part of food preparation at a party was usually a man's work. He laughingly admitted that "everyone" wondered if a European woman did a "man's work." We had some guests that were still at the party two days later, and learned that such celebrations are expected to last as long as food and drink remain. The success of the party tended to insure our reception in the village by helping to dispel some of the rumors concerning our purposes in coming to the community. We apparently ate, drank, and danced as "neighbors" were expected to do. Since it may take some time for a celebration to be arranged, the first weeks of residence in a community can involve a plan of work which will allow you to be seen as regularly and widely as possible, and which will provide details of the physical and social arrangement of the village. These aims can be met in mapping the community, making a household census, cataloging food and technology, and collecting genealogies. In the first days of residence, a scaled map of the village area should be drawn showing every structure of any type and the general physical features such as streams, springs, hills, ravines, and so on.[3] A map will provide the means for easily identifying property, neighborhoods, direction of community growth, and main routes of entrance and exit. It will serve as the basis for a census of population.

The recording of a census of names, ages, sex, family relationships, number of children born, number of children alive, and so on of each household in the community should follow the mapping work.[4] These data will contribute later to studies of birth, mortality, and migration in the local group. Although it may be possible during a population census to record the details of food and tools used in the community, it is probably more useful to revisit each household for a census of these items of daily life; a return

---

[3] For some references to map-making techniques see Debenham (1956). In some cultures the making of a map or conducting a census may arouse immediate suspicion and fears, and so, as with other techniques of fieldwork in the study of culture, the ways one proceeds are best governed by the facts of the local situation. There is no special formula for conducting a field study.

[4] Some references to and discussions of population study are to be found in Hauser and Duncan (1959).

for a technology and food census gives more opportunity to be seen and heard on an informal basis, and allows for validation and addition of data missed during a population census. A careful record of foods gathered, hunted, and grown, including those from domestic animals, and an accurate description of the inventory and uses of tools allow for some understanding of many behavior forms observed in the early period of research.

The collection of genealogical information is important for the understanding of social structure in a community.[5] These data can be combined with census information to determine relationships by descent and marriage between households. And these data can contribute to a more complete understanding of ideal and real social relationships between members of a society.

There are a variety of problems associated with census and mapping activities which must be faced as the work proceeds. It may be that a community defines certain areas to be out of bounds to strangers, or that some locations are not to be visited at particular times. In Sensuron the structure in which head and hand war trophies were kept and the burial grounds of the village were generally considered out of bounds to visitors. Rice fields could not be crossed at times of planting and just prior to harvest. Questions concerning certain Dusun family relationships had to be phrased carefully to avoid offending informants. Generally, Dusun will not use the kin term for their mother-in-law in ordinary conversation. And the direct elicitation of personal names is embarrassing to Dusun. Few persons in Sensuron know their exact ages. It was necessary to ask repeatedly for the name, age, and sex of persons not in the household at the time of the census. These problems were dealt with through asking for in-law data from older children, personal names fom parents or others in the family and in trying to find a series of local events which could be placed in a time scale, to allow estimation of birth dates. A rebellion, two locust plagues, four severe floods, three typhoid epidemics, two cholera outbreaks, and the Japanese occupation during World War II provided known historical dates for estimation of ages. A series of questions concerning the whereabouts of absent family members finally elicited full census data of family size and composition, including a grandmother locked regularly behind a bamboo housewall to keep her maniacal attacks from harming the family. In cataloging technology, it may not be possible to ask directly about certain items used in ritual or magical activities. In Sensuron there were a number of items of food and tools used regularly by male or female ritual specialists which could be talked about freely by everyone but the specialists; the first indications of the persons engaging in specialized ritual activities came in their refusal to answer certain questions during the food and tool census.

It may be that among the problems to be faced in these initial research activities will be the extra hospitality and good humor of the community. Dusun typically considered our first visits to their houses to be

---

[5] For recent discussions and examples of the genealogical method see Schusky (1965) and Romney (n.d.).

special occasions for eating, drinking, talking, and joking. While my mapping of the village proceeded without too much delay, I found that the population census involved working my way slowly from house to house, accepting food, drink, and elaborate introductions in each family. I learned quickly that the local rice wine was quite potent, for I accepted the explanation given me in each household that unless I drank two out-sized bamboo cups of wine as a toast to my mother-in-law she would lose her sight. After a week of my struggle trying to handle a strange language and strong drink, the village headman took me aside and explained that I did not have to drink two cups of wine to avoid my mother-in-law going blind, since this was a joke at my expense. I learned then of the local avoidance of the name or kin designation of a mother-in-law, and of the good time I was affording the village. I also learned I could merely touch my right index finger to any food or drink, while repeating a phrase of ritual acceptance and in this way avoid having to consume it. I completed the population, genealogical, and food-technology catalogue work rapidly after learning these items of Dusun behavior.

During the time of mapping and census work it would be useful to make records of and to learn the forms and meanings of body postures, gestures, gaits, and emotional indicators commonly used in the community.[6] It would be of help also to learn the forms for gift acceptance, greetings, exclamations of sympathy or wonder, the significance of the ways questions are asked, and so on. These data will provide a means for understanding behavior ranging from indication of direction through styles of affirmation and negation, to postures typically indicating relaxation, acceptance, resentment, or hostility. Familiarity with these ways will allow for their use in your work with informants. Care should be taken in the use of forms with special social meanings. In Dusun life any male not directly related to a younger man calls him "nephew" as a familiar form of address. The younger man is expected to use the term "uncle" in reply. It is a gross affront to use such terms with any inflection indicating ridicule or sarcasm. Until proper inflections are learned, English speakers may accidentally use the terms with an inflection of ridicule.

Routine of Research

After completion of these mapping and census activities, the daily routine of research will depend on the nature of the study and the style of local life. In a general study of culture, a regular routine of observation, interviewing, and recording of a number of topics (see Chapter 3) can be set without too much difficulty. More specialized studies, such as those of music, agriculture, or social organization, may require the setting of a daily research routine according to the availability of people and accessibility of

---

[6] See Birdwhistell (1952) for comment on recording data of posture, gesture, and gait. Fieldworkers must be willing to make errors in their efforts to learn postures, gestures, gaits, language, and so on. One must try in ignorance.

places. In either a general or a specialized study of culture, it will be necessary to adapt to the ways of living in the community. In Sensuron most people were up an hour before dawn, asleep an hour after sunset and followed work and leisure routines according to the agricultural cycle. Our observations of behavior and interviews had to be adjusted generally to these routines.

Our work day began at the same time as that of our Dusun neighbors, but ended after midnight as we finished the day's notes. The headman's pigs refused to move next door with him and got us fully awake each dawn as they squealed beneath our house floor. They were handy for garbage disposal. Our meal times had to be adjusted to allow us to be out in the community at the meal times of families, and our schedule of daily research had to be adjusted to the presence or absence of large numbers of people; during days of field preparation, planting, weeding, harvest, and storage of rice, the village was emptied of healthy adults from early morning to midafternoon. We knew it would be necessary to adjust to the fact that important people were busy and that observations of their behavior must be made in rice fields, with hunting parties, and during work tasks ranging from tree cutting to mushroom gathering or to weaving. One must also allow for time involved in unexpected events such as drownings, quarrels, accidents, shipwreck, death, and so on. One can expect that when he adapts his study to local routines and events, and then add to these demands the necessary transcription, filing, and ordering of notes (see Chapter 3) and his care of personal routine needs, that his days will comprise at least an eighteen-hour work routine. In the first months of study it is vital that at least one hour each day be provided for formal linguistic study with informants; even if you learn from 25 to 50 words a day, interviews concerning grammar and syntax are necessary. The first vocabulary to be learned probably should be the words and expressions concerned with illness and medication and emergencies.[7] We learned the usefulness of "there is a bad snake!" very early in our stay in Sensuron. When and whether you take a brief rest from this schedule depends on your own life style. For some, the pressures of a year of such a routine are welcome, for others regular periods of relaxation are necessary.

In the first month of research as mapping, census, and preliminary observations proceed, it would be useful to the conduct of general research in culture to select specific areas of the community for intensive observation and interviewing. The households about your residence can comprise a primary social unit for observation and interview. Several other areas of the community can be chosen as secondary social units for observation and interviewing. In Sensuron and Baginda the two primary social units comprised twenty-three households with a total of 116 persons. In Sensuron fifteen

---

[7] Medicines, surgical equipment, and dressing materials should be arranged in such a form to allow for their quick use to avoid wasting time and to provide for emergencies, especially those involving several persons.

households with forty adults and thirty-one children were the primary social units. In Baginda eight households with twenty-six children and nineteen adults made up the primary social unit. In addition to the fifty-nine adults and fifty-seven children of these two primary social units, 117 adults and fifty-eight children from five secondary social units served as informants and subjects for observation of Dusun culture in two communities. We resided in the middle of both primary social units with no more than thirty yards distance to the furthest household of either unit. In Sensuron our nearest neighbors were fifteen, twenty-three, and thirty-one feet away from our house. For two years in two Dusun communities we could see, hear, and ask about events of daily life occurring in 23 households. Our neighbors could also watch and listen to us. Your house should usually be as close to your neighbors as can be arranged. Little observation can be accomplished across a half mile distance. Secondary social units provide a basis for determining the accuracy of information gained in primary social units and allow for study of variations in culture in a community. Careful identification of the areas of a community for observation and interviewing is basic for systematic research, since such selection consistently focuses attention on a sample of the local population.

It is possible that some event, or combination of events, in the first weeks of study will make it necessary to terminate residence in a community and begin in another location. An outbreak of cholera, destruction of a staple crop through natural disaster, or the sudden death of a widely respected person are events that occur without regard for the anthropologists' interests. It sometimes happens that a stranger will come to be a scapegoat for events causing a community wide crisis. The hostility and social withdrawal of persons necessary for a study of culture can be overcome in time. In that event, since time and funds for research are often limited, it would probably be more useful to move to another community and begin fieldwork again. At the very least a selection of alternate residence locations should be considered and some general plans made in case it becomes necessary to change residence.

3

Observation, Interviewing,
and Recording Data

THERE ARE a variety of techniques used by anthropologists to gather cultural data. These consist of observing behavior, interviewing persons about behavior, and the systematic recording of data through use of notes, photographs, tape recordings, and the collection of objects. This chapter briefly discusses these means for research.

Observation and Interviewing

The setting of a study can affect the nature of all of the anthropologist's observation and interviewing.[1] It is helpful in making observations to try to live in a place where village activities tend to center, such as near the house of the community leader or chief specialist in ritual, the village square or church, or on the path to the village well, bathing place, main route to fields, or main road. It is useful to have living quarters constructed in such a way that rapid observations can be made from the house. In certain physical environments this will be difficult, but some arrangements should be planned for being able to see events of daily life as they happen. A fist fight or the quiet passage of important persons can sometimes be completed by the time you get out of your house. A porch or outside shelter of some type in which you can work and see about the area is a useful first base for systematic observation of culture. In our Dusun work we had centrally located houses with large porches and covered work areas outside to serve as points of observation. A regular routine of brief visits to the house-

---

[1] For some selected comment on observation of culture see Bateson (1941); Bell (1953, 1955); Bennett (1948); Herskovits (1954); Honigmann (1955); C. Kluckhohn (1938, 1951); and Mead (1931, 1933, 1946, 1956b, 1963).

holds in the primary social unit provides for a second type of observation. A plan for being in particular households for certain periods of time at specific times of each day gives opportunities to note routines and events of daily life. Such a schedule of visitation depends on your relationships with your neighbors and the local etiquette for visiting, but usually can be accomplished without difficulty if a daily pattern of visits is established and maintained. We regularly visited each household in our primary social units on a schedule which provided for systematic observations of each one over different periods of the day for a year of the Dusun calendar of work and leisure days. A third type of observation is based upon a regular routine of walks through the community. The routine of each walk can vary somewhat, but the times should be rigorously observed. In our Dusun study observations of behavior were made from slow walks through the villages just after dawn, before noon, and at dusk. Every second day a fourth trip was added to this schedule. This walk varied in time from midmorning to midafternoon and late evening. These walks provided an opportunity to observe the community routine and the occasion to ask about births, deaths, trips, arguments, work plans, rituals, and a variety of other cultural events which could go unnoticed without an effort to be out in the community regularly. As a year of residence progresses these three routines of observation can be extended through observations of important special events such as harvest, funerals, housebuilding, trials, and others. We tried to observe and ask about most special events in the community.

A fifth type of observation can be gained from the physical setting of your residence, which can be used by the community as a place to gather regularly for leisure time activities, for some community deliberations, or for playing by children and adolescents. In many societies people will tend to congregate near the house of an anthropologist during the first weeks of residence. Some indication of welcome, whether through offers of food or drink, by playing a short-wave radio, or by giving first aid, will promote a routine of behavior which can provide many opportunities for observation. In our Dusun studies as we regularly gave medicines in the early morning and late afternoon village leisure periods, we found an opportunity to hear the plans and discussions of events of each day. And we could carefully observe parents with children, as well as the actions of relatives, friends, and enemies. We provided places to sit, wood for fires, lighted a pressure lamp at dusk, and often played our battery-powered short-wave radio, tuned to the Dusun language broadcasts of the colony radio station.

The ways in which you observe behavior depends upon the style which puts you at the greatest ease and provides maximum information. Probably a combination of direct and indirect observational skills will become useful as you gain experience and knowledge of local culture. In many cultures some events are defined as private, although taking place in public, and therefore cannot be watched directly. You can expect that some forms of behavior may make you uncomfortable or uneasy when they differ greatly from your own culture's definitions of propriety, honesty, kindness, and so on. The first ritual killing of a water buffalo left us with a sense of unease as we watched the animal thresh about in its own blood. Whether you take notes as you make observations depends upon your sense of personal ease while writing, your concern at witnessing all details of an event, and your awareness of reactions in the community to obvious note-taking. If notes are made of observations, clear indications should be used whether the notes are made at the time of the observation or later, and whether statements by participants are quotes or paraphrases. In some cultures, public note-taking is difficult due to fears of records being kept of private events, whereas in other cultures little attention is given to the use of notes. The Dusun paid little attention to note-taking. It is helpful to be able to watch and retain a great amount of discreet data without making notes. It is useful to do a systematic study of your ability to remember certain types of data; checking a photograph of an event against notes written from memory is one means of making such a determination. On some special occasions too many different events of great complexity occur too rapidly to allow much time for writing. I found that watching a knife fight did not provide me with any time for writing notes, especially when we were called on to give first aid to both participants. The substitution of photography for note-taking is sometimes possible (see below). The skills of observation must be practiced. A cultural anthropologist must learn to see and retain great amounts of detail if his work is to be meaningful.

In the first months of a study the classification of observations will be difficult since meanings for and the functional interrelationships between cultural forms may be unknown until after lengthy interviews with many informants. An anthropologist must avoid classification of observations in terms of his own cultural experiences. If a man is observed beating a woman and the population census reveals that the couple is married, it would seem proper to file the observation as an instance of "wife-beating." However, you may become aware later that in the local community men and women generally agree that some sickness is best driven away through public flogging, or that women learn best when struck hard in public, or that married women must periodically show the strength of their husbands through suffering a public beating. If such meanings obtain for the form observed, classification under the heading of "wife-beating" is so misleading as to be a grave distortion of local culture. It may be useful in the first months of study to classify all observations you make in a series of *behavior types;* that is, acts observed which appear to have similar forms. Thus, each observation of a beating of a woman by a man could be filed simply as one type of cultural behavior. In the course of a year or more of observation, a series of behavior type classes will arise from systematic observations. From the data of such classes it may be possible to state the frequency of particular cultural forms and to identify persons specially associated with such practices. It should also be possible from these data to begin to understand special divisions of labor, the nature of social statuses, different role behavior forms, and the frequency of expression of special cultural forms.

Interviewing members of the community concerning behavior observed and classed into behavior types will provide a variety of meanings and functions for forms of local culture. Choosing a topic for interview from observations can be undertaken according to a plan to ask about behavior types most noticeable over a period of time or by talking about behavior forms witnessed during the day. In either instance meanings and functional interrelations for observed forms of behavior will begin to emerge from interviews in time. However, there will be a point when it will become necessary to make inquiry concerning forms of culture not observed. In the course of a year of systematic observation it may be, through special circumstances, that you can actually witness most behavioral patterns known and widely used in a community. It is more common that there will be many areas of culturally influenced behavior that will not be observed directly unless residence is maintained for many years. Thus, the form of the inauguration of an American president and the coronation of an English monarch could require different periods of observation varying from four to as many as sixty years. And there are aspects of human culture which cannot be directly observed.

At this point in research it would be useful to begin to choose topics for interview from one of the general guides for field study available to the anthropologist. The most commonly used field guides are *Outline of Cultural Materials,* (Murdock 1960) and *Notes and Queries on Anthropology* (1951).[2] The *Outline of Cultural Materials* contains some eighty general categories which are subdivided into about 633 topics, each of which contains between five and twenty specific subjects for inquiry. Field guides to the study of culture can provide stimulation to inquiry about forms of culture not yet witnessed but to be expected (housebuilding) or about aspects of culture not necessarily manifest in behavior (conceptions of guardian spirits, creator gods, beliefs of soul shape and location, incorporeal property values, and so on) but vital to understanding of local life. In addition to guides to general study of culture, there are a variety of field guides for study of special topics such as child-rearing practices, language, and others, which can be used as a basis for interviewing.[3] Where no field guides have been published for a specialized study, it is helpful to carry to the field several articles or texts on the subject which are generally recognized by anthropologists as contributing to the advancement of knowledge in that area. Topics for interview may be suggested in these professional publications.

---

[2] In addition to these field guides to study of culture, see Beals and Hitchcock (1960); Beardsley (1959); Hutchinson (1960); Keesing (1959); and Wolfe (1959).

[3] For a field guide for study of enculturation, see Hilger (1960). For selected guides to study of language, see Bloch and Trager (1942); Bloomfield (1942); Gleason (1955); Goodenough (1956); Hockett (1958); Hymes (1959); Lounsbury (1953); Nida (1945, 1947, 1950, 1957); Pike (1947); and Voegelin and Harris (1945).

There are several techniques of eliciting information during interviews.[4] Anthropologists ask direct questions concerning a topic ("Why do some married women wear a necklace of shell?"). Sometimes, as with topics considered in Dusun culture to be embarrassing or harmful (gossip for example, and magic) questions can be put in an indirect form of a general statement about some other persons ("Some people talk bad about other people doing this or that. What do you think?")

It is also informative to begin an interview with a broad statement concerning a topic, then allowing informants to talk as they please ("Agriculture seems important here. Can you tell me about it?"). It also is possible to get informants to talk in detail through asking them to give an event analysis of some occurrence in the community, and then recording their comments in verbatim form. The verbatim accounts provide a view of an event which is difficult to obtain through questioning. This technique has been developed by Fortune (1935), and Mead (1940, 1947, 1949), and is very productive of data. It was most useful in our Dusun fieldwork. Some informants will talk only if allowed to steer the interview to the topics of their interest; some will talk with little regard to the specific questions being asked from observations or through use of field guides. In our Dusun fieldwork we found some informants willing to talk about anything, at length, without prompting. The technique of interviewing on a topic while participating in the behavior can also be used successfully in some cultures. We worked as members of harvest groups in Sensuron and had an opportunity to ask specific and detailed questions of cultural form, meaning, and function. Although it can be very productive of cultural data, the participant-observation technique depends very much upon the personal characteristics of the anthropologist and the nature of the culture studied. There are a variety of opportunities for participant-observation in every society that should be utilized. It should be noted that observation and interview data can generally be obtained in most situations without participating fully in every cultural event. It will be necessary to select certain types of events to be studied in detail in a series which will be meaningful, such as birth, bathing babies, treating sick babies, rituals for babies, and so forth.

In addition to the techniques used, successful interviewing depends also upon the conditions of the discussion between the informant and the anthropologist. In some societies it is difficult to talk with one person alone,

[4] There is an extensive literature concerning interviewing, relations with informants, and determination of validity of data. For some selected comment, see Adams and Preiss (1960); Becker and Geer (1957); Blum (1952); Casagrande (1960); Dean and Whyte (1958); Dollard (1935); Hallowell (1956); Lewis (1953); Malinowski (1922); Merton, Fiske and Kendall (1956); Paul (1953); and Whyte (1960). For some contrasting views, see Evans-Pritchard (1952); Firth (1957); and Piddington (1957). The development of methods for study of culture can be traced in the writings of Boas (1920); British Association for the Advancement of Science (1852); Frazer (1916); Kroeber (1939, 1957); Linton (1936); Lowie (1953); Radcliffe-Brown (1958); Radin (1933); Richards (1939); Spencer (1954); and Tylor (1906).

for a group may always gather. This was typically true in our Dusun work. There was always a background of noise. It was often too warm, damp, or windy for a lengthy discussion of a complex topic. Dusun onlookers have the habit of inserting nonrelevancies, or turning the conversation in a direction more interesting to them. Sex, age and prestige often became involved when a Dusun informant answered questions in front of others. Women would not talk about childbirth before nonrelated males, adolescent boys did not want to talk about their games before young men for fear of being held childish, and most informants did not wish to appear to be questioning the status of a senior man or woman among the onlookers. If special definitions of manners for asking or giving information exist, as they do among the Dusun, knowledge of such practices may help to give meaning to cultural forms.

Interviews will often be interrupted by events beyond the control of the anthropologist. If the topic seems vital to understanding the culture, some specific means of returning to the talk should be arranged before the interview is interrupted. Arranging a time and location for continuation of the interview will help provide continuity of a topic through time. It is useful to keep a list of questions on topics to be discussed at the time of a next interview with an informant. It was not unusual for a Dusun informant to grow tired, bored, or defensive as he talked and to want to break off the conversation. Learning to detect these signs and to recognize that more information can be obtained in other interviews is important. Many experienced fieldworkers limit interviews to one and two hours with any one person in a day. Special occasions such as an opportunity to talk with an infrequent visitor or a ritual specialist may make it necessary to hold an interview for a longer time.

The accuracy of data is important. Observational data are distorted through the inexperience of the observer and physical and cultural limitations of his perceptions of events. Interview data are also distorted through the mechanisms for defense of the ego in operation in every human group and due to randomly distributed differences of capacities for learning and insight in a society. Human beings in every culture rationalize, project, and sublimate their desires, wishes, and fears. And these processes of ego defense operate according to the intellectual capacities of individuals.

It is not unusual that particular rationalizations will be shared widely in a culture. We had to take into account among the Dusun that the members of the community, without regard to their intellectual capacities, consistently misled us concerning property, avoided talking about aggression while being highly aggressive, openly boasted of sexual conquests while actually being conservative in sex activities, but gave precise, accurate, and consistently truthful answers to the most difficult questions on religious behavior. We found that one way of determining the accuracy of Dusun cultural data was the identification of the ego-defense processes widely shared and used in that culture. Another estimate of accuracy can be obtained in the phrasing of similar questions to a great variety of informants in the primary and secondary social units. We regularly asked the same questions of different key informants over a long period of time and then compared their answers. Still another kind of judgment of accuracy can be gained through seeking to determine the internal consistency of data from one informant; the same questions repeated over a long period and in a variety of interview settings can elicit answers which tend to show the accuracy of an informant. We were able to determine the validity of most of our key informants' comments by this means. A fourth type of estimate, and perhaps the most useful in a general study of culture, can be obtained in careful matching of the statements made by informants concerning their behavior and the actual behavior type record for the person. It is not uncommon for informants to note that they would or would not behave in a particular way in a certain situation. Thus, Dusun men will note, "Men never strike their children." When a long-term record of observation, which shows several instances of Dusun males striking children, is matched to such statements, some idea of the accuracy of data is gained. It is also not uncommon for informants to behave regularly in ways they do not, or cannot, discuss. The relating of data of behavior types to interview data provides for some determination of accuracy of cultural data in a manner which may bring you full circle to widely shared ego defense processes. If many males insist they do not strike their wives, while behavior type data shows the opposite to be true, the evidence is strong for the existence of a cultural rationalization. Another technique is to ask informants to give a retrospective account of an event you have witnessed and recorded in detail. This provides a way of learning about the kind and accuracy of recall characteristic in a society. Mead (1940, 1947, 1949) highly refined this technique of determining accuracy of data. We used it extensively in our Dusun field study.

Key Informants

The identification, selection, and use in interviews of persons occupying important status positions in the primary and secondary social units, the community and area is of great significance in a study of culture. Most members of a community do not know the full repertory of forms, meanings, and functions of their culture. Women know aspects of culture men do not know well, or at all, and vice versa. Ritual specialists and political leaders have learned ways not known to others. Children know children's games, songs, jokes, and riddles better than adults. It is vital to be able to identify all persons occupying key, or vital, status positions in the community. At the completion of a general study an anthropologist, having systematically observed and interviewed key persons in a community, should ideally be possessed of more knowledge of the culture than any one person in the group. The observer should come to know the aspects of culture experienced by the hunter and the potter, ritual leaders, village herdsmen, children, the aged, the adolescent, the blind, the crippled, and the alcoholic. The anthropologist must make an effort to know both the widely shared aspects of the culture and those known only to a few persons. It is generally true that individuals occupying key status positions which must be earned (that is, holding *achieved* rather than *ascribed* status) have an acute awareness of details of culture known to persons holding other key status positions. The behavior type records of key informants also give indications of the ways important people are occupied over long periods.

It is very helpful to be able to select a key individual in the community as an assistant in research. It is even more useful to have a key informant working as a member of your household. However, in many communities the possibilities are very limited for finding a key person who is free and willing to work as a research assistant or as domestic help. Yet, there are circumstances in which it may be possible to have someone in your household who either has occupied or will come to occupy a status of importance in the community. In Sensuron we identified and selected a girl of sixteen for our household assistant. Her grandmother was one of the leading female ritual specialists of the Tambunan area. The girl had been trained as a ritual specialist. In addition, she was closely related to six persons holding key positions in the community. She served as a key informant in Sensuron. Her special ritual knowledge and her ability to give meaningful and accurate details of widely shared aspects of her culture were invaluable. We regularly had advice on household and research matters from three primary social unit neighbors who were key persons in Sensuron: the village headman, a senior female ritual specialist, and a very aged and renowned warrior. Their roles in looking after our comfort, health, and safety became intertwined with their key status activities. As we came to depend on their advice for household affairs, we found it easy to talk with them concerning their special knowledge of Dusun culture. Their confidence in us and our trust of them, when added to our close relationships with our household assistant, provided a basis for work with most other key persons of the community.

The identification and selection of key informants available in a community may take some time to accomplish, since your knowledge of local culture must be sufficiently advanced to be able to recognize the vital status positions and you must have established personal relationships in your work that will allow you to approach such persons for their help in the study. By the end of the second month in residence, as behavior type observation and interviewing proceeds, it would be useful to have compiled a list of all key status positions known to you, and to match these with the names of persons holding these positions able and willing to act as key informants. As you inquire concerning behavior type observations, it is likely that informants will readily identify persons holding key statuses in the community. It may even be that individuals holding key statuses will identify themselves and volunteer their services as informants.

The elicitation of assistance from both ordinary and key informants, requires thorough awareness of the subtle rules governing social relationships between members of a culture. The manner of deference in address to older persons, the definitions of politeness in asking direct questions of a non-relative, the regulation of physical distance between sexes, or styles of inferior-superior social relationships, all bear upon success in gaining co-operation of informants. Key informants tend to be even more aware of such nuances of behavior because of their special status. We were often reminded of our Dusun "manners" by key informants with comments such as "The right way to speak is. . . ." It should be possible to add this knowledge to aware-ness of body posture, gesture, gait, and emotional indicators learned during the first period of fieldwork to be able to deal effectively with key informants in most situations. It is unwise and unethical to try to trade off the informa-tion gained from one informant in hopes of getting more data from another person. The maintenance of relations, especially with key informants, de-mands that the anthropologist maintain a discreet silence about very personal interview and observational data, and try not to be drawn into personal dis-putes between key people of a culture or between government officials, or between officials and the community. Make notes of the content of any dis-pute, but do not allow yourself to be brought into the argument as a tale-bearer, advocate, or judge. Enough hostility comes to focus upon a resident stranger in a community without attempts at personal manipulation of informants, especially those of importance in a society. Personal protection should be extended to informants in all publication of data, since comment given in confidence should be respected. There is no logic to the supposi-tion that since particular informants are not literate, publication of confidential material would not be harmful. An anthropologist's responsibility to his informants and hosts is to protect individuals and communities whenever possible from harmful allegations or reprisals.

It can be expected that your relationships with some key informants will be closer than with others. This is a natural consequence of living arrangements, work habits, and a disposition to "like" some informants more than others. It is helpful to try to avoid showing open favoritism to any key informants. A rapport that has been established through a slow build-ing of confidence and exhibition of hard-won knowledge of social rules can be easily destroyed through seeming to publicly favor one key informant over others. At times, it is difficult to balance the demands of several key informants for special assistance or extra attention. On occasion, it is even necessary to break off a close relationship with a key informant that appears to be causing harm to general feelings of trust built up with other key informants. In such instances, it may be advisable to take a brief break from residence in the community. A week or two away from residence may serve to terminate social relationships no longer advantageous to the research. On return to the community, there should be an opportunity to establish a different pattern of dealing with key informants. And such a break in residence can be utilized as a time for review of notes, making plans for further observation and interview, and setting a schedule for special studies. It may be advisable to take a rest at the end of two or three months of research, even if there are no problems of dealing with informants.

It is possible that identifications of some key informants will be in error. It is not unusual for an anthropologist to attract persons seeking to improve their status through association with an outsider, especially one appearing to have some power with the local government. All communities contain persons playing roles not appropriate to the status positions assigned them. Most anthropologists have had the experience of sorting out the informants really holding key positions. Until you have determined accurately the status of each key informant, there must be some reservation concerning data recorded.

Use of Interpreters

The decision to use an interpreter to assist in the course of observation and inquiry is a crucial matter that can affect the course and nature of research. Cultural anthropologists are usually trained in the techniques of recording and analyzing an unwritten language. It will be necessary to learn to carry on a conversation concerning ordinary daily events if you reside in a native community for a long period. If the culture is one that has not been studied and if there are no descriptions of the language available, it may be necessary to undertake to record and analyze the language in order to learn it well for ordinary conversation. A manual for the beginning student on this subject should be particularly useful here (Gudschinsky 1967). A series of spiral notebooks with ruled pages are helpful in making language records. Each notebook should be numbered. Each page can be blocked off in a series of sets of four or five numbered lines; on the first line you can record by use of the International Phonetic Alphabet the verbatim comments of the informant. The second line can comprise a literal translation, while a third line can be used for a running translation. One or two other lines can be used for linguistic analytic comment. All notebooks and linguistic work should be recorded in a diary. In some culture regions, a "trade," or *contact* language is used; in Borneo simple *Malay* is used for trading, in Melanesia Neo-Melanesian ("pidgin") is spoken, while in East Africa *Swahili* is widely used. In some areas, English, French, Spanish, and Dutch are used as contact languages. Learning a contact language before going to the field will assist in making residence arrangements and dealing with officials, village leaders, and community members. And a contact language can be used as you begin research. If there is no generally used contact language, it will be necessary to use an interpreter to establish residence and begin the research. Even if an interpreter is used during the first months of residence, a concerted effort should be made to learn and use the local language. The skills of learning a language vary among anthropologists. Some learn native language rapidly and quite well, others find it difficult to proceed quickly to a high level of proficiency. It is important that you rapidly learn to carry on ordinary conversation despite the availability of an interpreter. If a contact language has been learned and can be used in establishing residence and in the initial period of research, it is still important to try to learn the local dialect for use in every-day conversation. Men speaking different languages may very well live in different worlds of reality. The structure of a language is a means of dealing with experience. In learning a language with a different structure than his own, the anthropologist comes to understand many of the ways reality is classed and used in a culture. The learning and use of ordinary conversation in a native language will sharpen appreciation and give access to the world known to a native community. For instance, the Dusun use the same term for the green of tree leaves and the blue of the midday sky. The difference between green leaves and blue sky may be "seen" but their language ignores this difference.

If there is any question concerning your access to or ability to learn the specialized vocabularies of different status positions, that is, the language of the headman in a trial, or that of a ritual specialist in a divination, it would be wise to seek and use an interpreter for interviewing. Although mastery of ordinary language provides awareness of categories of reality used in a culture, it may not provide for the proficiency necessary to obtain complex information in specialized areas of life. In Dusun society ritual specialists use language not generally heard in daily life, and emphasize double meaning in the special language; a word not heard ordinarily carries two meanings. One is a general meaning, sometimes known to ordinary persons, the other is a meaning shared between the specialists and supposed to be known to the spirits called on in ritual acts. The use of ordinary language will not usually be sufficient for interviewing key informants concerning special aspects of culture. While ordinary conversation will provide preliminary data in most areas of culture and perhaps extensive information concerning some areas of culture (for example, living routines, building, tools), it may not be at all sufficient in dealing with areas of culture in detail which may be emphasized by a community (for example, religious belief and practice, property, kinship, law).

If an interpreter is from the society being studied, he can be of great help in interviewing on special topics. If an interpreter is from another society, it is helpful to select someone speaking the contact language as well as you do. An interpreter will not speak your language as well as you do, and it is unlikely that you will learn to speak his language, if he is a member of the society, as well as he does; in a contact language you may be on similar terms in speaking equally as well. An essential requirement of communication is equality of comprehension of a language between speakers. If the interpreter is not a member of the society, it would seem preferable to have him fluent in a contact language rather than halting in your own language.

The selection of an interpreter should be undertaken with some care. If it is possible to secure the assistance of a person practiced in the skills of interpreting, it will save some time in training him for research. It will usually be necessary to train an interpreter to your definitions of the tasks of interviewing. An interpreter must be reliable in his rendition of your inquiries into the native language and in giving replies of informants. Until your command of ordinary conversational language is gained, you will be dependent on the interpreter's sense of integrity, responsibility, and honesty in his tasks. This will especially be so if you must put your inquiry in a contact language for an interpreter to translate to and from a local language. It would be useful to seek to gather references locally from government officials, traders, missionaries, and community leaders prior to employing an interpreter regularly. The final selection of an interpreter must depend on your estimates of his skills in his tasks of translation, his awareness of the importance of the tasks for your work, and his reception in the community. It usually takes a long period for the anthropologist and interpreter to adjust to each other's ways of proceeding with an interview. A properly chosen, trained, and reasonably alert interpreter can himself begin to provide access to special cultural data after a period of six months or so.

Some anthropologists use interpreters as general field assistants. The assignment of tasks other than interviewing to an interpreter must depend on the place and prestige accorded to him in the local culture. Field assistants can ease some of the burden of observation, interview, and general details of living. An interpreter must have the ability to successfully undertake other tasks which may involve him in different ways in a community. Unless you are confident of an interpreter's capacities and have some awareness of his local status, it may be advisable not to assign him the role of general assistant in the research. In Sensuron my interpreter was a respected senior member of Dusun society, extraordinary in his ability to learn, possessed of great integrity, and capable of a high level use of Malay. He resided in another village but was available regularly for interviewing. I felt it demeaning of his status in the society to ask him to take on other duties as a field assistant. As noted above, I found we had the assistance of neighbors for many details of living in the community. In Baginda I employed a very reliable young Dusun man also competent in Malay to act as my interpreter and field assistant. I came to depend on his help in a variety of activities in the research and the tasks of daily living. Both men are well known and respected in these communities and were able to conduct detailed interviews after a very brief period of training and practice. My verification of their work showed it to be accurate, direct, and possessed of detail that I could not have obtained in most circumstances.

Some of the problems arising in the use of interpreters have been noted above. Perhaps the most important point of contact you may have will be your interpreter. His style of representing you may come to affect your work. If he fails to observe language conventions and manners used in everyday social relations, and is dishonest in his contacts with informants, he will hamper your work. If he dislikes female informants or children, your work may be distorted. If an interpreter argues with informants, you may lose contact with key persons of a society. Perhaps the most effective solution to these problems is to try to learn ordinary language well enough to be able to monitor directly the comments of the interpreter, and so to determine his effectiveness and the place of the prestige accorded him by the community.

Anthropologists seem rarely to employ women as interpreters or field assistants. Many female anthropologists have employed males in these tasks.[5] It seems that most communities more readily accept a man in the role of an interpreter and field assistant. There are good reasons, however, for using a female interpreter. Research on child-rearing practices, women's sexual behavior, economic and special craft activities will often be studied more efficiently with a woman interpreter acting as intermediary with key female informants.

Recording Cultural Data[6]

Anthropologists generally try to preserve the wholeness of cultural data. They treat the complexity of culture as a fact and proceed on the assumption that the trained observer, with his sharpened insight and rapid perceptions, can try to deal with the complex nature of culture until more efficient methods for analysis of structural complexity can be developed. For the most part cultural anthropologists communicate the essence of complexity in culture through word portraits based on field notes. Those with greater literary and artistic skills have been more successful in providing a sense of the wholeness and complexity of human life. However, technical developments of the past forty years through refinements of cameras, film, lighting, sound recording, and devices for analyses of film and sound tape make it possible now for the less artistic and literary cultural anthropologist to supplement his field notes by visual and auditory means, and thereby extend his ability to tell of the richness of complex material.[7]

Until recently most anthropologists have lacked the technical and manual skill to deal with mechanical aids for treating complex cultural data. The primitive state of equipment and low budgets have usually forced them to use a single still camera and a limited series of still photographs to show

---

[5] In a recent series of essays by twenty anthropologists (Casagrande 1960) describing their interpreters, field assistants, and key informants, only two women were portrayed, and one of these by a male, although four of the accounts were by female anthropologists.

[6] The first part of this discussion is drawn from some comments by Margaret Mead (1956a).

[7] An extensive treatment of photography in anthropology is to be published by Collier in 1967. For other discussions, see Bateson and Mead (1942); Collier (1957); and Rowe (1953).

major informants, village scenes, and major types of artifacts. This is changing rapidly as it becomes increasingly obvious that detailed photographic and sound records greatly enhance systematic treatment of complex cultural data and as research budgets have begun to be approved to include costs of extensive use of technical aids. The use of large numbers of photographs, many in rapid sequence, on the order of 30,000 per year of study, allows for quantative analysis of cultural data. For example, it is possible to draw from a large number of photographs the frequency of the use of a particular gesture, posture, or facial expression or to determine the anxiety of children in particular situations. Large numbers of photographs make it possible to develop and check new hypotheses after leaving the field. Analysis of our Dusun photographs shows infants carried on the backs of mothers with their heads generally turning to the left, rather than the right which was more usual from studies in other societies. The most important function of large numbers of photographs is to allow the observer to check the distortion of his observations because of his own cultural experience. If a large number of photographic sequences of interpersonal behavior are made immediately after entering the field, it is often possible after formulating hypotheses to return to photos made before the hypotheses were articulated. In returning to the pictorial detail of the situation that may have given rise to an insight, the observer can check his inclination to distort cultural data in the direction of his own cultural learnings.

Motion pictures have a natural superiority over candid camera action photographs. However, a semiskilled photographer using a still camera in rapid action can provide photo detail generally equal to that obtained through a motion picture camera used by a novice. Motion picture films are much more expensive and are more difficult to analyze in the field, since complex equipment and a rather high degree of technical skill is needed to produce an analysis that could be obtained more simply through spreading hundreds of still photos on a flat surface. Records of cultural complexity made with still cameras seem today to offer the best means of providing contrasts between culture regions (as between Africa and Oceania) and over long periods of time in the study of one culture by different observers. Our candid photographic record of Dusun culture will be usable twenty-five years from now by another observer. Motion picture films will not be as easily studied, unless some device is developed to allow the simultaneous viewing and analysis of three or more films.

Large numbers of sound recordings made with lightweight battery-powered tape recorders provide for much data on the richness and complexity of a culture.[8] Linguistic studies may be based on permanent tapes

---

[8] Discussions of uses of tape recorders in the study of culture are to be found in Nettl (1954); and Pickett and Lemcoe (1959). It is not uncommon that a field-worker making a special record of cultural data, or studying a particular and limited problem, will take few photographs or make limited tape recordings. And the personal feelings of a fieldworker may also limit use of such devices in study of culture. Some fieldworkers do find it difficult to use cameras and tape recorders out of a concern for their informants. Such concern is, of course, quite legitimate.

of conversations recorded in natural settings. Tape recordings should be made of sounds with emotional content, such as women addressing children, men arguing, funeral wailing, as well as the content of everyday background sounds, such as the calls of domestic animals and noises of work tasks in and near houses. Analyses of linguistic and other sound data can provide for a means of inquiry into the world of reality known to members of a culture and are most valuable for checking accuracy of data at a later time. While it is very expensive and time consuming to tape record every interview, there will be particular interviews with key informants on vital topics that can be taped for future playback. And talking a description of a rapidly developing and complex event into a tape recorder may be more satisfactory than trying to write notes while observing.

Generally, it is best to purchase simple and well-tested cameras and recorders, which require little maintenance and will hold up for long periods of use under difficult climatic and work conditions. An expensive and complex camera that jams because of rapid use or fails due to dust, cold, or poorly made parts is of little use. If a budget permits, it would be helpful to carry into the field at least two recorders and two still cameras, with a wide range of lenses. Provision should be made for loading film in the field, and supplies for the care of cameras, film, tapes, and recorders must be secured before setting up residence. A generous supply of plastic containers and bags, with a good supply of strong rubber bands will aid in keeping camera and recording equipment dry, dust free, and away from high humidity. In the tropics it is necessary to have a supply of small plastic bell jars with attached hand pumps to establish a vacuum for control of humidity and avoidance of fungus growth. In our Dusun studies we also stored camera and recording equipment in large, heavy plastic containers with tight seals. Such containers are used in American kitchens for purposes of storing flour, sugar, salt, and so on. Across the bottom of each container we placed several inches of fresh silica gel and covered it with a piece of gauze material. The silica gel was replaced twice a week; the previously used gel was cooked in a large frying pan over an open fire and allowed to cool in a special plastic container, then re-used. If the more efficient bell jars are used, a supply of plastic bags that can be sealed will help in keeping equipment sealed off once taken from the vacuum storage. Cameras and tape recorders should be carried on trips wrapped in several sealed plastic bags to keep off the rain and dampness. Even after a fall in a river our cameras have remained dry. One of our still cameras has been used in two field trips, taking at least 10,000 photographs, and shows little signs of wear. It would be wise to take a limited amount of equipment to test-develop a roll of film from every camera each week to avoid loss of great amounts of film and vital observations due to fungus on lenses, light leaks, and so on.

Extensive developing of photos in the field should be undertaken only by the experienced. It is expensive to mail negatives from the field for developing and printing, but it will save spoiling vital film because of ineptitude. It will also save time to have the work done commercially. Unless you can have someone devote a good deal of time to the work, field developing can occupy great amounts of time better invested in observation and interview. It will save considerable funds to buy film in bulk and to cut and load it in the field, using modern lightweight daylight-type loading equipment which is now generally available.

If films are developed commercially, it may save time and expense to have sheets of contact prints sent to you by mail for review. Full prints and negatives can then be sent to persons receiving copies of your field notes, or arrangements can sometimes be made in the nearest town or city for storage in a film vault. We stored black and white and color negatives and prints for a time in the cold storage room of a firm in the North Borneo capital, then arranged to have negatives mailed directly to the United States after commercial development in Singapore and Australia. Sheets of contact prints and prints were mailed to us and were used to edit and collate photos with field notes. It is vital that detailed records be maintained for each roll or sequence of film with each set of prints, and that negatives be put in a system of notation as to location, date, time, participants, and your impression of the major feature of action ("divination," "rice harvest," and so on). The careful notation of the time of all observations and interviews provides one way in which cultural complexity can be organized for analysis. Without time notations on notes and photographs, data can become meaningless, as the search for particular observations or comments becomes more demanding, the more frustration will be felt in the hours spent searching for an item which could be simply retrieved through a time note. Prints can be cross-indexed from time notations, so effort will not be wasted in looking for "an old man chopping wood," or a "mother teaching a boy to walk." If retained, prints and negatives should be protected in the field from dampness, dust, and insects. After indexing each film, it probably would be helpful to store materials in a closed container.

Since the basic means of recording data still is through use of field notes, it would seem useful to anticipate procedures and problems involved in the making, classifying and using notes. A typewriter is a valuable aid in recording notes in a permanent form. Selection and purchase of a well made, lightweight typewriter, and arrangement for shipment to you of expendable typing supplies (ribbons, carbon paper) should be part of the preparation for long-term field study.

Field workers have reported a variety of ways to make, copy and analyze and file field notes.[9] I have a preference for writing my notes of observation and interview in longhand on "note sets." I have found that it saves much time to make up sets of seven pages of second sheet paper cut

---

[9] Some comment on the different ways of making, filing, and analyzing field notes can be found in Richardson (1960); and Sturtevant (1959).

to 5″ x 8″ in size and with carbon paper inserted between the pages for duplication of the original page. My notes for a day would consist of forty to sixty sets (240 to 420 total pages) each numbered in sequence.[10] My files are ordered in such a way as to allow me to classify the content of each original page according to the location of behavior or interview, persons present, time, date, and the behavior type or interview content represented in the notes. An example of a page follows:

68 Day—Rain: 59°F TRW *Diary of Events* 3 Oct 59 Sat. Sens. P 1

7:05 A.M.—*bAlAtAk* is sifting padi on porch. *L* comes out of house with five *tengAs* over shoulders, calls to her 2 year-old da playing in mud in front of house, *"kAdA-dA! ooiA! gEmuLi!"* Muddy girl climbs house steps, mother kicks her tail with instep as she runs across porch; Mother goes off south on path 3. *S* comes down way toward our house dressed only in a loin cloth, despite pouring rain. Goes to his 4 yr.-old great grandson (*G*) who is playing in mud by our hse. porch, grabs him up by the left arm, and without a word drags him bumping along ground to porch where he is deposited with a thump! *S* goes in house. 7:10 AM: *K,* 8 yr.-old male of house 3 comes on to porch, squats, urinates off porch in an arc, and watches. *M,* his 9 yr.-old sister comes out, watches, then hikes up sarong, squats in same place as her bro. had been, looks out over yard, asks bro. something I cannot hear; bro. sticks tongue out sharply. *M* arches a stream of urine out into yard, then rotates her pelvis in a manner to cause arc to swing from side to side. *K* says something I cannot hear. *M* gets up, pulls her sarong over her head, thrusts her pelvis sharply forward. *K* runs in house. *M* drops sarong, runs in after him. 7:15 AM:*bAlAtAk* finishes sifting, goes into house.

—Daily Routine—Childhood activities—Techniques of enculcation—Sensations—Misc. Sexual Behavior—Language—*bAlAtAk*—*L*—*S*—*G*—*K*—*M*

I file the original pages of each set, which are numbered in the sequence in which the notes were written, as part of a "daily diary" section. I place the remaining six carbons of notes for each set in the specific behavior type classifications of local culture, according to the content of the page. I then write a separate set of anecdotal notes to be added to each day of daily diary notes. In addition, I keep a general diary of events as a broad index to our work and events in the community. I note the page numbers and dates for each day's note sets, anecdotal notes, and linguistic notes in the diary. I also make comments concerning theoretical clues, the state of our health, mail sent and received, and books read. I also kept a "noise record" to follow the patterns of sounds of life in the community. At the end of any

---

[10] It should be noted that the total pages in a note set is a function of the size of handwriting; my sets are numerous because I write in a manner to fill a 5″ x 8″ page in a half a dozen sentences. This procedure of note-taking has been developed after suggestions of E. H. Spicer of the University of Arizona.

period of residence I could read through my daily note sets, anecdotal comments, and diary in the sequence of past events and research, or turn to a specific category of a behavior type and have immediately available in one place the notes from all observations or interviews. I found this system of great aid in reviewing my work and in rapidly seeking specific items of information already reported. It is vital that you keep a separate record giving full details for any abbreviations used in any notes. Fieldworkers of long experience report, and it has been my experience, that writing notes of observation and interview is a function of whether or not there is a rapid series of major events in the community: a birth, followed the same day by an accidental death, a trial for theft, and a house fire, or even three births in two days. It may be difficult to write full notes on each event. Most experienced fieldworkers follow the practice of writing up the details of the event not witnessed previously, and cross-referencing the differences in the other events with similar ones already recorded. It would be useful to not try to write too many notes. Experienced fieldworkers report being bogged down by an overabundance of note detail, made while sitting for five hours waiting for an important event, such as a ritual, to begin. Again, notes cross-referenced for differences with observations already made can contribute to solving this problem. It is extremely useful to keep a single page face sheet of an event when you have no time to record it in detail to allow a return for a write-up in detail later. The face sheet should, at least, note participants, location, time, date, and major events in the observation. It is of help in the field not to allow yourself become a victim of your system of note taking and filing. To reduce frustrations, borrow from experienced fieldworkers and be alert to new ways of dealing with cultural complexity.

Provision should be made for care of notes while in residence and for their maintenance in case of accident. We shipped 6″ x 9″ x 12″ fiberboard file boxes to the field for use in filing notes. If you follow a plan of using note sets, at the end of a year of residence, there may be some 5000 or more pages of notes cross-filed in a large number of file boxes. I have regularly placed my daily diary, anecdotal and other key notes in a light wooden case made to a size of 4′ x 6″ x 10″ and equipped with a set of carrying handles, hinged top, hasp, and lock. In this way, I could easily transport the originals of observations and interview notes as I traveled by road, plane, or ship. The danger of fire was great since we used open fires to cook and pressure lamps in a bamboo house with a palm-thatched roof. The wooden case could have been thrown out a window with little delay and damage to vital notes. Anthropologists have lost most of their field notes through fire, theft, accidents in boats, and so on. It would be useful to make some provision to always have one set of notes readily available in a form for easy transport. As noted above, it would also contribute to the security of your notes to periodically mail a copy of them to someone at a point outside of the area of residence. And care must be taken that rain, dampness, insects, and mold do not damage notes. In Borneo, we followed the practice of keeping the fiberboard note boxes covered with individual plastic bags sealed with rubber bands. We regularly had heavy monsoon rains driving through the bamboo walls and leaking through holes eaten by bugs in our palm-thatched roof, and had an abundance of paper-eating bugs.

The writing of rough field notes, even when made in spiral notebooks, is usually accomplished under difficult conditions. The anthropologist often finds himself sitting on a house floor, or on the ground, squatting in the mud, or standing and talking while watching some event. It helps to be able to write on a firm surface during observation and interview. I have found it useful to write using metal clipboards with spring covers, of a type used by field engineers and construction men. I have had a pencil and a pen attached by string to the clipboard. These boards provide a hard surface for writing clearly onto all carbons of note sets, and give some protection from rain, mud, and wind, and accidents similar to one in which I dropped my notes through the bamboo floor into the pig wallow beneath the house. The clipboard should be kept ready for use at any time; at night, it is wise to have a flashlight or lantern ready for use in writing notes.

It is not unusual that anthropologists will find few records of the physical environment or studies of the biology of a population. In such instances, it is necessary to make provisions for recording systematically such phenomena as the amount of rain or snow fall, daily temperature and humidity ranges, and the direction and speeds of winds.[11] Gauges, indicators, and thermometers for accurately recording these events cannot usually be obtained in the field. If it is apparent that local records of climate will be insufficient for your field study, it will be necessary to order simple recording devices before going to the field, and to plan a routine of daily observations. In Sensuron, we made a systematic record of rainfall, humidity, temperature, and wind speed and direction by setting times each day for collection of these data. If physical anthropological data are to be collected from the local population, instruments such as sliding and hinged calipers, scales, and so on should be sent to the field. Observations of stature, weight, body proportions, skin color, and hair shape are best made according to standard practices and with usual devices for recording such data (*cf.* Montagu 1960). If special studies, such as blood-group typing, physiologic functions, and others are planned, provision must be made not only for recording devices, but also for the special ways required for handling material from the field, such as preserving and shipping blood for typing.

Special studies may require use of other devices for recording data. Research concerned with the ways a society exploits the natural environment may involve analysis of soil types, and classifications of plants used and animals hunted. Studies of metallurgical practices, basketry, textiles, pottery making, dancing, musical instruments, or making and uses of hunting poisons may call for special devices for obtaining, recording, and analyzing

---

[11] For references to making physiographic descriptions and records of climate, see Lahee (1961); and Great Britain Meteorological Handbook (1956).

such data.[12] Special studies of sense-mode functioning in a cultural milieu will require use of complex devices for securing data (vision and color charts, tuning forks, and others).[13] Many studies of the interrelations between personality and culture utilize special devices and tests to allow informants to talk about, or "project," their personal needs in a verbal form. Projective tests and devices are complex in nature, require skill and experience to use meaningfully and some intensive training to "score" or analyze for generalization.[14] Children's drawings of persons and events are often important adjuncts to use of projective tests. Whether a general or special study of culture is planned, if a need for use of special aids in recording data can be anticipated, it would be helpful to plan for securing and using aids that seem likely to be most productive.

The collection of data on material culture provides an opportunity to learn the ways tools are made and used to exploit the natural environment, and to make other tools.[15] In a society which has not been studied previously, it would be useful to the conduct of research to collect samples systematically and send to a museum most aspects of movable material culture (for example, weapons, containers, farming or fishing utensils) well identified and tagged in the field, and to try to witness the making and use of all larger items of material culture (houses, granaries, boats, and so on). The census of technology conducted in the initial period of residence should provide a base for rapid collection and a long-term study of cultural objects. Depending on your budget and time, it would be informative to make detailed film records of the sequence of work by several craftsmen in the making of some types of common material culture, with a tape recording of their explanations for each step of the process. It would be useful to have models of objects, or a diorama, of some key event, such as harvest or divination, made by an important participant. In the event of a model or diorama being made, photographs of the full-sized object or event should be filed with the ex-

---

[12] For discussions of soil types, see Millar, Turk, and Foth (1958). References to classifications of plant and animal life are to be found in Archer (1945); British Museum Instructions for Collectors (1932–1954); and Fosberg (1960). For discussions of ecology, see Bates (1953); Thomas (1956); and Malinowski (1935).

For some discussions of metallurgical practices, basketry, pottery and textiles, see Barrett (1952); Coghlan (1954); Bunzel (1929); Shepard (1956); Black (1957); and Reichard (1936). For some discussions of dancing and music, see Kurath (1960); Densmore (1936); Karples (1958); and Nettl (1954).

[13] For comment on methods of study of color perception, see Ray (1952).

[14] For discussions of projective tests in studies of culture, see Adcock and Ritchie (1958, 1959a, 1959b); Henry and Spiro (1953); Henry (1955); and Spindler (1955). If use of projective tests is planned in fieldwork, take as many types as possible to the field to allow a greater choice of methods. Some tests are too expensive to allow spare copies to be taken to the field; it is useful to carry details of ordering and descriptions of these tests. Many tests can be ordered only by psychologists. Hence, some arrangements have to be made to secure tests you will need. Take equipment (scissors, cardboard, drawing tools, crayons, and so on) to allow you to construct tests if you need to do so.

[15] For some examples of collection and descriptions of material culture, see Buck (1930); Haddon and Hornell (1936–1938); and W. C. Bennett (1949).

amples, with notes on the person making the object. A range of all styles of manufacture should be collected, to show poor as well as superb craftsmanship. Collection of designs and styles of decoration of pots, baskets, and other objects is also important as a base for later studies of culture change, and in relating patterns in material culture. The complete repertoire of one major craftsman should be recorded and gathered if it is at all possible.

Travel for Comparative Study

In the first chapter it was noted that travel in the general region of the study is an aid to making decisions about residence. While in residence, trips to nearby communities will also provide data for comparisons of vital aspects of culture. In areas where separations of local groups have lasted for very long periods, due to factors of geography (mountains, rivers) or social practices (warfare), minor differences in language, physical type, or custom assume major significance, both to the local groups and a visitor. These differences have led to the classification of local groups, by their own definition, and by those of outsiders, as belonging to separate "tribes," "races," and "languages." Travel about the region will provide impressions and data regarding physical, cultural and linguistic affiliations.

Only travel to other communities in the area can reduce the confusion of claims made by local people, by government officials, and found in previous literature of the people and area. It is helpful to travel only after the initial collection of data has been completed and you have a solid foundation of knowledge for comparative studies. Although comparative travel will not always allow for specific answers concerning affiliations, origins, and migrations, it is useful to have such data for purposes of evaluating claims made by natives and others.

4

Choices of Status and Role

OST ISOLATED NATIVE SOCIETIES have difficulty in finding a social position, or status, for a stranger taking up long-term residence.[1] The anthropologist comes to live in a community with an interest in most things that happen in the lives of the people, from talking about and witnessing events ranging from childbirth, and hunting, through pottery making to planting of crops. Community leaders are rarely concerned with witnessing and inquiring about children's games or talking about proper ways of behavior for a newly married woman. Women do not generally concern themselves with problems of making and using weapons. But the anthropologist makes an effort to know something about these and other kinds of culture known in a society.

False Status-Role Assignments

It is to be expected that the varied activities of the anthropologist will be talked about in the community, as an effort is made to find a status for him that will fit his many and different roles. In the course of such discussions, a number of statuses will be proposed for the stranger which seem to fit his actions. Depending upon the degree of a community's contact with and hostility to other cultures, the anthropologist may be falsely assigned initial statuses of government informer, tax agent, policeman, or missionary. The phantasy of individual natives may produce stories that the anthropologist is a cannibal seeking a new supply of flesh for his people, or that he is the

---

[1] For a discussion of the ways human societies react to the resident stranger, see Robert Redfield (1953: 9,33), and Philip Newman (1965). See also the comments of A. R. Radcliffe-Brown (1913: 150–151) on his problems of gaining admittance to a settlement of Australian Aborigines.

incarnate form of a feared supernatural being, or even the long-awaited savior of the community from defeat in war, sickness, and death.

False status-role behavior assignments can greatly disrupt the initial period of study. When an anthropologist is widely suspected as a government informer, adults of a community will tend to avoid him if they fear punitive acts by government forces. Children may hide at the sight of an anthropologist reputed to be a feared supernatural or a cannibal. If he is said to be a savior from the ravages of misfortune or disease and death, work may become difficult due to the efforts of people to gain his personal attention. Solutions to these problems vary with the society and the experience of the anthropologist. One reason for holding a celebration for the entire community during the beginning period of residence is to enable as many persons as possible to see personally that the phantasies about the anthropologist are inconsistent with the facts of his acts and appearance. A community celebration will not eliminate, but only narrow, the number of false status-role assignments being made in a community. It is sometimes possible to follow a celebration with an attempt to create and introduce the status of "anthropologist" in the social structure of the community. The status accorded to a person asking numerous questions concerning many events can sometimes be more easily understood by a native people if the fieldworker can take to the field texts that contain material from studies of culture in the local culture area or region. Pictures of your own relatives are very useful in learning kinship terms and uses, particularly if the photographs can be passed about while you listen to the discussion. From this discussion it may be possible to learn of statuses in the local society. Showing pictures of babies at different developmental levels helps to ease fears of cameras and photographs as harmful. If the texts are well illustrated, contain linguistic material somewhat familiar to the local community, and have photographs of an anthropologist at work, then it may be possible during the initial period of residence to use such materials to begin creating a status. During censuses of population and technology, full opportunity can be given in each household for everyone to look at and talk about the text and photographic material. It may also be possible for the anthropologist to assume an existing status in the native society to create a place for his activities in the community. Occupying a known status in a society is more likely to give an accurate view of local culture than trying to be a "visitor" for a long period. Traders resident in native groups long have followed the practice of seeking adoption into the status of a relative to leaders or economically powerful members of the society. Some societies have traditionally made strangers prove kinship with someone in the society or face expulsion (Radcliffe-Brown 1913). An anthropologist can deliberately seek permission to hold a known kin status while doing his study. While the ideal behavior associated with the status of "uncle," "cousin," or "relative" may not permit observation and questions of persons engaged in a wide variety of acts, it is possible to begin a study of culture from such social positions. In instances where there is secret knowledge aasociated with several statuses, such as being initiated by a men's society, or a magical specialist, and in hunting, it will be very difficult to have access to all data for all of these positions. It would be more useful to assume one status and to acquire full detail of all secret knowledge associated with it rather than try to straddle several such statuses. Generally, the pattern of secret knowledge is the same for all statuses of a society. It may be effective to try to hold local kinship status and at the same time to create a role as anthropologist by systematically explaining what one does. In this way the new status and associated role behavior can be created from a base of expected behavior forms.

Many anthropologists prefer to go on recording data while allowing false stories to die out from lack of credible evidence to support them. A community will soon tend to discount the more obvious untrue status-role stories. Whether the student of culture sets out to create the new status of "anthropologist," or deliberately adopts a kinship status and chooses to ignore all but the most damaging rumors and tales depends on his experience, knowledge of local culture, and insight into the dynamics of ego defense mechanisms. It helps to develop skills of recognizing the subtle ways societies protect themselves from resident strangers.

Adoption of any status which is not consistent with the aim of openly observing and recording a culture can create grave difficulties if the fraud of status assumption is discovered by the community. And the ethic of science is ill-served by fraudulent methods of study. If it is clear at the outset of a field study that it will be necessary to tell falsehoods about the purposes of residence and work in a community, it would be best to go to another place to avoid compromise of the value that science is a public process, honestly discussed and conducted. Trained anthropologists do not try to obtain data under the pretense of false status assumptions. Most societies can find ways of incorporating the anthropologist over a period of time providing the people are given an opportunity to search out positions to fit his roles, and if they are frankly and patiently assisted to understand the ways a student of culture must act.

The Anthropologist and Culture Change

There is involved in the establishment of status-role another question of vital importance. The anthropologist is an example of an often quite alien culture system. He serves as a model for new ways of acting and thinking about old problems. When it was obvious that I did not hesitate walking through muddy places while a rainbow shone in a brilliant arc across the horizon, my Sensuron Dusun neighbors remarked openly concerning my lack of fear of the evil supernaturals waiting there to "eat my souls." When we treated most illness, wounds, and burns as matters demanding routine care and treatment over a period of days or weeks, our Sensuron neighbors were faced with a sharp contrast to the Dusun tradition of dealing with sickness, accident, and misfortune through one divination and curing ritual which could not be repeated for fear of admitting failures in dealing with supernatural beings and forces. These and many other contrasts between our ways and those of our neighbors provided a setting in which Dusun were constantly comparing their traditional ways with those of the resident anthropological strangers. We were continuously asked about our ways of doing things. It was not unusual to have a Dusun informant counter my question on a topic with a detailed inquiry concerning the way our culture dealt with the issue. When I asked about childbirth, I often found it necessary to talk in detail concerning American practices of treating birth and infancy. I was asked to give explanations of crop planting and harvest, styles of house building, conceptions of justice, time, honesty, and incest, and spent hours in free give-and-take on the interest of Europeans in omens. We could have refused to discuss these matters, and chosen not to have given any medical assistance. In doing so, we would have cut off a valuable source of Dusun cultural data, for we were learning the extent and nature of Dusun concerns with their own cultural system and the ways individuals dealt with new ideas. In talking as friends about our own ways, we were providing for the Dusun much the same experience we were gaining from living in their society. Our study of Dusun culture gave us information which highlighted and accentuated the ways our culture deals with problems involving nature, social relations, and the conceptions of the supernatural. The inquiries about and observations of us by our Dusun neighbors provided them with information to compare and contrast our ways with theirs, and often raised their level of awareness of their own culture. Field study does involve a reciprocal interchange of cultural information. The anthropologist serves as a model by his very presence in a community. His actions influence the culture he studies, whether or not he intends to have such influence on local life. He will be imitated while he is feared. He will be queried while he is being given information. Sometimes changes in local culture appear directly as a result of only the physical presence of the anthropologist. The presence and comments of the anthropologist concerning his own culture can set the stage for accelerating a change already occurring in the local culture, and the anthropologist provides through his presence and comments material for later consideration of change in local culture. We induced change in Sensuron simply by our presence. In order to obtain drinking water that would be healthier than the supply from the nearby river, I asked the village headman to have forty-foot lengths of bamboo split in half, cleaned out, and tied as gutters under the edges of our bamboo house roof. I led water from the bamboo gutters into old kerosene tins, and later into a used gasoline drum. We obtained enough rain most days to give us adequate water for drinking and cooking. When we arrived in the village, our neighbors carried drinking and cooking water from the river in sections of bamboo up a half-mile steep slope. They were used to making complex wood and bamboo flumes and conduits for transporting water across ravines and gullies for irrigation of rice fields, and knew the technique of transporting spring water through bamboo down hillsides to houses for drinking and cooking purposes. Our solution to the problems of carrying water and to maintaining our health were responses to a situation which affected our work. Several of our Dusun neighbors soon followed my plan for catching and storing water, and improved on my design through more efficient uses of bamboo for transport and storage of rain water. This change in Dusun culture took place without comment or direction by us. We provided a model to follow and improve upon. When I returned to Sensuron two years later, I counted more than twenty systems of house gutters in which I thought I could detect a similar plan to the one we had introduced.

A process of change in Dusun culture was contributed to by our concern and comment on the need for treating illness systematically. Younger adults responded readily to our suggestions that babies with diarrhea be given water, with salt added, at regular intervals to prevent death from dehydration. Older adults paid little heed to our requests to give babies water regularly or bring them to us several times a day. According to the records we kept in our residence in Sensuron, there was a sharp differentiation between responses of adults under thirty years from those over that age with respect to repeating medical treatments. By the end of the year of our stay we found that more older adults were returning to have wounds and burns redressed and to obtain more antibiotics. Our concern in this instance obviously contributed to acceleration of a process of change already at work in the culture; many younger adults, from contact outside of the village with colonial and missionary medical services, were aware of the need for repeated treatment of illness and wounds and were prepared to change the traditional form of behavior. Our model contributed to acceleration of a process of change in Dusun culture.

The anthropologist must be fully aware of his role and must not confuse his status as an observer and interpreter of culture with that of the agent of directed and induced culture change, such as a government officer or missionary.[2] The research anthropologist's task is to study culture, while recognizing and acknowledging that he contributes to change by his very presence. His responsibility is to weigh carefully any deliberate choice he makes to aid in, or direct, change. When the anthropologist moves from a primary concern for recording and understanding a culture system to actively directing change, he assumes a very different status. He becomes an agent for directed culture change, an applied anthropologist, concerned with imposing and implementing goals and values he feels desirable. In this status the anthropologist uses cultural knowledge for particular ends. Any choices made to assist in the life of a people whether it is in working as a member of a harvest group, giving medicines, or simply showing people advertise-

---

[2] For comment concerning deliberate intervention in a culture by an anthropologist, see Holmberg (1955).

ments from popular periodicals involves the problem. It is obvious from the illustrations and comments here that we made some contributions to change in the culture we were trying to study. We tried to examine and talk regularly about our assumptions in doing these things. Our decisions were not based on values that would perpetuate a particular sectarian religious creed, or one political or economic system. Nor were we trying to promote change simply to see the consequences of our introductions. In trying to make explicit our cultural biases and learnings before we introduced any change in Dusun culture, we were engaged in holding in check our inclinations to react to the poor conditions of life that our American cultural perceptions made obvious all about us each day we lived in Dusun villages. Our adherence to the ethic that our task was to learn and record Dusun culture provided a balance to the temptations to interfere, advise, and direct local events.

Role Relations with Informants

It can be expected that in the course of working closely with informants for more than a year, there will develop a series of reciprocal social relationships that will become doubly contingent; that is, the anthropologist will be expected as a friend to return the time and effort spent by an informant.

Three problems can occur in development of such expectations. The first is one of "assigned" cultural change, the second is the question of the appropriate ways to return the courtesies of time and effort given by informants, and the third is that some informants will want to protect the anthropologist from learning the "bad things" of local life. Informants may even take upon themselves to introduce change in local culture in the name of the anthropologist. We found one key informant giving directions in our stead for cleaning up the debris about the houses, telling people of better ways to plant rice, making demands everyone build latrines similar to ours, and implying we wanted our friends to become Christians. It took some time to persuade the informant we did not want to interfere with Dusun life and to gather up the tag ends of the many assignments given for change. It is probably useful to be alert to the innovator in culture seeking to use your position to further their own concerns, whether from a genuine desire "to be like" the strangers or out of other motives.

There may be direct or implicit demands by informants for the anthropologist to loan tools, food, money, and transportation, to provide gifts; and to give payment for services. We were regularly asked by Dusun to lend our tools for their work. We were asked to provide rice and meat for several families who said they were unable to pay the high costs of borrowing rice for the few weeks until harvest. We were requested to give many loans of small sums, and even to pay a jail fine for the oldest son of a key informant.

We were asked to use our Land Rover for rides at odd times of the day and night, for medical emergencies, by wives fleeing a beating by a husband, and by drunks on their way to another party. Our house was a regular stop for travelers coming out of the mountains to trade with Chinese merchants in the small shops on the center of the Tambunan plain. Many mornings we found a party of people sleeping on our porch, or waiting to be fed before going on their way. Our porch seemed to be the most convenient location for passers-by to duck in out of a rain shower, and the Land Rover a comfortable place to take a nap, carve a knife handle, or just pass the time of day. The tires of the vehicle were interesting to listen to as the air was allowed to escape. I often pumped one or more tires up, usually with much comment on the art of that process from the culprit. I had one informant who would regularly let out the air from a tire and then would borrow the pump to reinflate it. We responded to most demands by informants for loans of money by refusing to meet them. Our explanations that honoring such requests would change our position in the community were generally accepted.

We learned to know when we were expected by an informant to return a gift of greater value than one given to us. We would often be given small portions of deer or wild pig meat from a jungle hunt. If the cut of meat was one considered a choice one, such as a liver, or a section of ribs with abundance of fat, we knew we were expected to provide a gift for the informant's services to us. We would then have to make discreet inquiries of neighbors concerning the nature of the gift expected in return. For the most part, such items were small, such as a box of shotgun shells, a pipe, a piece of cloth, or a bead necklace. Occasionally we found we were being asked for a gift of considerable value. We always attempted in these instances to find the reasons for such a request. One old man, aware that he was dying, wished to buy goods to arrange for an appropriate funeral. A mother of a baby near death from tuberculosis was desperately trying to raise the cost of a traditional curing ritual, while an old warrior wanted a trip in the airplane he saw flying over each week. In most instances we tried to arrange for the gift through securing the goods desired or by giving some equivalent.

In some cultures informants will expect to be paid in cash for their services. It probably is desirable in this case to set a monthly fee for all informants and to maintain it at that level during the study. Any variation may cause disputes between informants and difficulty for interviewing. Gifts can be given in addition to a regular cash payment if it is felt appropriate and desirable. It is unwise to underpay or overpay informants. A good practice to follow could be to try to determine the monthly cash income of a village family, compare that with a wage paid by the local government for laborers and clerks, and strike a balance somewhere between these points of income. Whether informants are rewarded for their help with gifts or in cash, or both, it is helpful to the conduct of a study of culture to know and use the details of courtesies of payment that prevail locally. It is of great assistance also to understand beforehand that most informants will come to expect that you will respond readily to their giving time from their concerns, even to the point of borrowing your equipment, making themselves comfortable in your house, or trying to be helpful in ways ruinous to equipment and supplies and even frustrating to your purposes of study of culture.

There will be some instances in any study of culture when informants may seek to protect the anthropologist from aspects of local life considered "bad," "evil," or "harmful." To have an informant seek to protect your sensibilities and feelings is to be paid a compliment as a friend, and to have such protection offered can provide valuable data concerning definitions in local culture of offensive or brutalizing events and practices. We found some of our Dusun informants and my interpreters trying to protect us from knowledge of many sexual activities and from facts of economic exploitations. In several instances my wife was given "ideal" information, that is, what was expected behavior, while the same informant gave me "real," or actual, behavior.

Usually informants will tend to lessen their protection of the anthropologist as he demonstrates his skills at language, participates in some local activities, and reacts calmly to learning "shocking" information on witchcraft, incest, cannibalism, head hunting, rape, theft, murder, and cheating among relatives and friends. It is helpful to practice watching yourself watch and listen to informants when information is given which does shock or startle you. It may be possible to at least check a look of consternation, horror, or disgust. I found self-control of this type valuable when, during an interview with a Dusun mother, for instance, she picked up her six-months old baby after he had defecated on the house floor, laid him across her knees, then called the five family dogs to lick his buttocks and anus clean, or when the village headman suddenly swooped up and castrated a passing dog while continuing to quietly tell me of kinship terms for cousins. Informants will be responsive to your reactions to events they view as "normal." Those among them that try to protect you from knowing the "worst" of local life may be especially sensitive to your first responses of dislike, vexation, shock, and fear. Some practice at control of overt expressions of disgust prior to field study may be very useful in a setting where many things shock and repel. And while it is impracticable for every anthropologist to undergo a series of extensive psychoanalytic sessions, it would be helpful to try to recognize some of those events that may cause the greatest personal reaction. Field experience in several cultures usually provides the anthropologist with an accurate conception of the events which cause him most concern.

Status-Role Relations with the Larger Society

It is likely that an anthropologist will have fairly regular contact with members of other ethnic groups in the capacity of government officer, trader, missionary, and traveler. These persons are important to the conduct of fieldwork because they very often are the only links between a native society and the larger society. Few of these persons can be expected to know the work of an anthropologist or to understand the delicate balance of status-role relationships that must be maintained through the course of much research. Some of these persons can seriously disrupt a study. Some local government officials sought to have us act as an adjunct to government services in dispensing medicines and collecting taxes. A few officials tried to capitalize on our supposed power and prestige with the distant central government through giving us unsolicited favors that disturbed our social relations with the Dusun community. Other local officials exploited friendship with us from sheer boredom and loneliness of duty in an alien place, or because of a desire to turn us against the Dusun. We experienced difficult situations in Dusun villages with intoxicated government officers and had several instances of local government officers of other ethnic groups who attempted to use our local status as a device to extract information for police purposes and to secure personal favors from informants. We became aware of the fact that some local officials were breaking the law. Their awareness of our knowledge of their illegal activities caused them to search diligently to find instances of our breaking regulations. It is wise to be discreet concerning your awareness of bribery, theft, conspiracy, misuse of position, and so on.

The general solution to such problems is to maintain contact only at an official level with those officials reported locally to be likely to cause difficulty. Most communities have made fairly accurate judgments of non-native local government officials and can give information about potential difficulty. Natives often have to suffer being cheated, mistreated, and lied to by local administrators. There are situations of field study where officials are friendly, eager to help, and worth confidence and trust. Our experiences with a number of petty, intoxicated, or brutal officials were more than offset by the personal kindness, unstinting cooperation, and genuine understanding of our work shown by other officers.

Contacts with missionaries in the area of study can cause difficulties. In North Borneo some Protestant fundamentalist evangelical societies operated with values that resulted in the abandonment of villages and the dissolution of native society in entire regions. Catholic missionaries maintained a more selective approach in their activities. Although we are not Catholics, we were seen as friendly persons by mission priests and welcomed at local missions and given much personal assistance in setting up our residence in

Sensuron. Our contacts with Protestant missionaries were tinged by their suspicion of our purposes and aims, and a fear that we wanted to locate and maintain a village representative of traditional "pagan" Dusun culture. In general, the extent of contacts with missionaries must depend upon judgments concerning the attitude of the missions toward native culture and missionary understanding of the nature of cultural study and analysis.

Relations with traders can be maintained only at the level appropriate for the local prestige of the individual merchant and his ethnic group. A small overseas Chinese community operated some shops near the center of the Tambunan plain. Many of the Tambunan Dusun fear and distrust Chinese and avoid Chinese merchants whenever possible. We were regularly asked by our informants to intercede for them with Chinese merchants said to be cheating or failing to pay for services given by Dusun. We generally avoided entering such disputes.

Most anthropologists have contacts with travelers from other ethnic groups. The presence of an anthropologist in a community may become widely known in a short time. Among Europeans and Americans this fact is sometimes taken to mean an open invitation to visit and look at "natives." We had about one European or American visitor every two months in the course of our fieldwork with the Dusun. Our isolation seemed no problem for the two New Zealand women school teachers trudging across the middle of the North Borneo mountain jungle, nor for the English mountain climbers walking to the nearby 13,455 foot Mt. Kinabalu. Some of our visitors asked us to find a "warrior with a freshly cut off head so we can take pictures," while others wanted us to stage a rice harvest scene in the months after harvest. We were requested to "have the natives do something exciting" and to "find pretty girls without blouses for color pictures." In some instances our visitors were sensitive to our place in the community and were understanding of our polite refusal to cooperate in the staging or arranging of any events. Other visitors left in an angry mood because of our lack of cooperation with their concerns. We had difficulty from some of these visits since the European and American women sometimes appeared in the shortest of shorts, and men insisted on being unshaven. Our knowledge of Dusun manners told us that a woman with bare upper thighs was offensive and exciting in such display. And we knew that all evil and cannibalistic Dusun supernatural beings were felt to have very hairy faces. More than half the male visitors we had wore thick beards. We had difficulty explaining our reasons for refusing to walk with these visitors through the village. Yet we considered bluntness preferable to loss of our evolving status-role position in the community. It is to be expected that you will offend some visitors by frank explanations of your reasons for not catering to their wishes for novelty or sightseeing. That risk is well worth the effort put into choosing and developing status and role behavior in the study of culture. It is a courtesy to extend your hospitality and to give assistance to visiting colleagues and other scientists. We had visits in our Baginda research from a junior colleague and his family, and a physician. Your professional obligations to such persons depend very much on their interests in your work; the junior colleague was undertaking field research in another North Borneo Dusun community and had been our house guest in the United States for a week while talking about methods of beginning his doctoral study with the Dusun, reading our field notes and records, and studying our photographs. His visit in the field was a part of our general invitation to use our data freely in his study. The physician came to us on the recommendation of a senior colleague to experience some of the things an anthropologist does as he goes about his work. Many of his professional interests are parallel to ours, and so we provided him opportunities to accompany us in observation and interviewing, while talking about field study methods.

5

Termination of Residence

THE EFFORT AND ADJUSTMENT necessary for a community to incorporate an anthropologist usually results in a permanent place being made for him in the society. When it becomes known that plans are being made for concluding research and leaving, there is likely to be a time of considerable upset in relations with informants. Most anthropologists have experienced the deep concern and genuine sense of loss manifested by their interpreters, informants, and friends when announcement has been made of the intention to return home. Although it may have been carefully explained at the beginning of the research that the fieldwork involved staying only a year, or eighteen months, an atmosphere of permanency almost always evolves. This is especially so if the anthropologist is successful in finding and occupying a key status in the community. His neighbors and friends may have come to depend on his presence and varied activities as a meaningful part of their own existence, for his work is involved with the simplest and most solemn moments of human life. In a year or more of research the anthropologist will be present at the births and deaths in families he has come to know well. Since he concentrates on being aware of everything that happens about him from quarrels to love affairs, from debt settlement to sickness, the anthropologist comes to know details of personality often unnoticed and unappreciated even by close relatives or friends of informants. As he lives for a long period and works as a human being among other human beings, the anthropologist comes to know that the culture he learns and records is delicate, complex, artistically pleasing, personally renewing, and as intellectually moving personally as any of the great achievements of individual artists or writers of his own culture. In reaching these profound realizations of the essence of being human in an isolated society, the anthropologist usually comes to impart to the community a sense of his belonging in their lives, affairs, and plans. When you have allowed someone to witness the most intimate and moving events of your life, there exists a bond that transcends the seemingly insuperable barriers of race, language, and culture. And so it may distress informants and native friends when the announcement of planned departure is made. It is well to make specific plans to lessen the emotional stress which may be caused through such an announcement, both for the sake of the continuing study in the time left and because it is a human obligation to do so.

Preparations for Termination of Study

A key decision to be made in termination of research is whether you plan to return to the community for further study. It will ease emotional upset for informants to say you will return soon. But unless you have such plans, it probably is not helpful to informants to make such comment, since the time will come when it will be obvious that your plans will not be carried through. When a decision is reached concerning plans for further study in the village, arrangements can be made for systematic termination of research.

Arrangements for disposal of equipment and physical facilities differ with respect to your intent to return soon, or to do no more work in the area. And responsibilities to key informants vary with your plans to return to the community.

Each culture has patterned ways for dealing with severing of personal relationships, whether from temporary absences, such as journeys, or from permanent separations due to intense personal conflict, divorce, or death. Special ritual forms and language are often involved in these acts. In the course of making plans to terminate research, it would be helpful to employ the detail of the forms used in a local society to deal with severance of personal relationships. In our study of Dusun culture we made a special effort to spend several hours with each key informant talking about our plans to terminate the study. Then we arranged for the performance of rituals by female specialists at celebrations to which our informants were specially invited. We were given gifts of magically endowed objects to carry with us to protect us from harm, and we made a donation of property and money to the headman to be used in paying costs of a divination for determination of the origins of any illness or misfortune caused by our leaving and absence from the community and to support a celebration at the next harvest. Wealthy Dusun families ideally provide such a feast each harvest time.

Responsibilities to Key Informants and Interpreters

It would seem an obligation to tell each key informant and interpreter personally of details of plans for leaving the community. And depending upon the closeness of your relationships with these persons, it would be well to try to anticipate the best ways of dealing with dependency needs established by them. We had to convince at least two older neighbors they could live on without our personal administration of vitamin and aspirin. Several mothers came to us extremely worried about the health of their infants, and one female ritual specialist was depressed because she was certain we would become sick and die when we returned home. The village headman was unhappy for weeks because we no longer would give him increased status as our mentor, protector, and close friend. In each of these cases, and others like them, we had to use our knowledge of the personal character of each informant and of Dusun culture to lessen the dependency on us that had grown up during our research.[1] It is time consuming to make such efforts, but it would seem an obligation of the anthropologist to try to leave as little emotional debris from his work as possible. This is especially so in the case of interpreters.

Interpreters are often "transitional" or "marginal" persons in their society; that is, the qualities and skills which make them most valuable to the anthropologist are often peripheral to the central values and activities of the native society. It is well to remember that your work with and through an interpreter has given him a new status, confidence, and influence in local society, while building at the same time a complex web of dependency relationships which can only be fulfilled by the anthropologist. The quickness to know and to value in an interpreter may be of little value to him in local life. It is doubly difficult for interpreters to accept the fact of termination of research and to continue working efficiently when faced with the loss of friendship, protection, and perhaps the first understanding of their intellectual gifts that they have ever received. Some effort to insure continued support of interpreters would seem in order, whether through seeking another position for them, or in making some provision for their economic security. We had no need to make a place or provide support for our interpreter in Sensuron, since he was already an important person in local society. In Baginda we tried to reduce the emotional stress of our leaving through assigning our house and furnishings to our young interpreter and seeing that he had funds to purchase land.

Disposal of Equipment and Facilities

Anthropologists collect a variety of equipment and facilities that must be disposed of on termination of research. If plans have been made to return for further study, then arrangements must be made for interim care of equip-

---

[1] Most anthropologists and their families feel sorrow and some experience grief when they must leave their friends in a community. It is very difficult to remain aloof while a part of the fundamental and commonly human events of birth, illness, accident, and death. The impact of these events on your friends will probably draw you into a bond of understanding and empathy which can transcend great differences in language, culture, and physical type.

ment and facilities. If there are no plans to return, then some equitable way of disposing of these items should be arranged and announced to the community. In Sensuron we distributed, or promised, to our key informants those things we did not wish to keep. The task of disposal was very difficult, since much of the material was considered in local terms to be of some value. The village headman had rented his house to us during our work, so we left him our few items of rattan furniture and small kerosene stove. We gave our kerosene pressure lamps and supplies to key informants whose help had been especially valuable. Our empty wooden boxes, kerosene tins, and gasoline drum went to others. We held a neighborhood party to finish the remainder of our food supply. Some items of household equipment were given to the nearest Catholic mission for their help in our work. We were puzzled concerning disposal of our latrine until the village headman suggested it be made community property and maintained for European visitors; three years later it was still in good repair and in use by the occasional European visitor to the village. While decisions for disposal of equipment and facilities may not be difficult in some communities, for the Dusun the acquisition of property as a gift is a considerable mark of prestige. And so careful estimates had to be made of the impact on informants of each crate, pot or tin given as a gift. Despite our care and good intentions we learned that a village court hearing took place three months after we left Sensuron concerning our precise intentions in giving a gasoline drum to one informant rather than another. If plans are made to return to a village, it probably would be desirable to ask the village leaders to help decide on an equitable form of distribution to avoid problems with informants on return.

Termination of Relationships with Members of the Larger Society

It is useful on termination of study to spend about two weeks to a month systematically retracing the route of contacts established when the work was begun. Calls on and discussions of the research with local and central government officers can establish, on their part, a sense of your responsibility for your impact on local culture. And any formal questions by the government can be dealt with directly, rather than allowed to linger on in exchanges of overseas correspondence. You may be able to repay research help given by the government with advice on affairs such as health, culture change, population, and so on, which does not violate the confidence of your informants, and can assist the government to help the local society in many ways. Final visits to the local merchants and missionaries who provided information and assistance in setting up residence will be a matter of simple courtesy and can provide some perspective for comments made by such persons after a year or more of your life in a local culture. These visits will provide opportunities to deal with any rumors or garbled stories concerning your work. Most anthropologists have had the experience of hearing wild tales concerning their activities that derived from false status-role assignments during the initial period of research, or of listening to rumors concerning their supposed acts circulated by unfriendly government officers, missionaries, or merchants. It may come as a great surprise to hear that you have been on a drunken orgy for a year, running about naked, or have been poisoning rivers and streams, promoting atheism, or cheating your informants of their family heirlooms. The surprise will be the greater when you know that your relationships in the village have become a secure, warm interchange between friends. It is usual that another anthropologist will hear such stories about a colleague's earlier work in the area. It would be wise to ignore such rumors and avoid passing them along to anyone. Such stories can cause great professional and personal harm to a colleague, and to you for repeating them to the detriment of a fellow anthropologist. It is likely that you will also be subject to such tales, to be heard later by a junior colleague. One way to deal with such tales is to ignore them as phantasy that will expire in your absence. Another is to try to stop them from doing harm at the level of officialdom where permission must be secured for return to the country if you wish to continue the study. Few senior government officials will believe such phantasies, but it is just as well to talk out the sense of "trouble" that derives from such ego projections on to you and your work. It probably is useful to anticipate that no matter how careful, discreet, and judicious you have been, you will be the target of rumor, phantasy, and denigration on the part of nonnative members of local society. Few anthropologists escape such stories.

Maintenance of Contacts on Leaving the Field

The anthropologist often maintains contacts by mail with interpreters and some key informants after leaving the field. We write to our Dusun interpreters and follow the practice of occasionally sending small gifts to them and several key informants as tokens of our continued concern for their well-being.[2] We derive some return from the contact in the form of letters giving continuing perspective on local affairs, but generally this is of secondary concern to our effort to support Dusun whose effort and understanding of our aims made possible our research in their community. We have tried to answer inquiries from our Dusun friends as promptly as possible, since we view these as an effort to maintain friendship with us. While such support is sometimes a burden of time and effort, it is deserved. And since anthropologists do return to restudy communities after twenty or twenty-five years, maintaining contacts after leaving the field provides for continuity over the span of a new generation. We have become aware from letters that our time

[2] Gifts are recognized in most societies as one of the standard forms of establishing and maintaining social relations with non kin.

of residence in Sensuron is marked now as "the year the white woman lived here," and that the babies delivered by us are named for us. From our time of residence a set of Dusun twin boys are called Tuan ("Lord" or "Master") and Tom, at least one little Sensuron girl is called "Land Rover," and a little boy is named after our portable radio.

Finally, the anthropologist has an obligation to try to make it possible for his colleagues to conduct other studies in the community or region. Actions that would detract from this possibility should be avoided, particularly those involving spreading of rumors and tales. It is a professional obligation of the anthropologist to be aware of and responsible to the colleagues who may follow him. Many anthropologists have had to bear difficult situations because of stories about purported actions by colleagues, or persons purporting to be anthropologists, many years before. Many studies of culture remain to be completed in societies about the world. It is a responsibility of the anthropologist to his professional peers and present and future students to conduct and terminate his work in such a manner to make possible other research in the society by the fieldworkers to follow him.

6

Some Comment on Method

The Completeness of Cultural Data

It has been noted that anthropologists seek in their research and their reports to preserve the wholeness of culture. When the community studied is small the experienced fieldworker soon comes to know its people and their environment well enough to sense by a shift in the level of everyday background noise or by a change in the attitude of his hunting companions that something of importance probably has occurred. Changes in noise levels can indicate, for example, that a water-buffalo fight may have injured someone, or a quarrel has resulted in one of the men going amok and injuring neighbors. A disagreement over shares of a deer hunt or a land boundary dispute may have led to changes in social relationships which, in time, can affect nearly everyone in the village. In the study of culture nothing in the life of a community can be wholly neglected. This fact raises the problem of whether any field methods used can ever result in a complete recording of everything in a culture. It seems physically impossible for a single observer to see, hear, and note everything occurring in a community of 500 persons. But however sketchy some observations may be, they must be handled systematically, and in this way the culture can be studied as a whole. Mead (1963:604) puts the matter in this way:

> If one does not map every taro patch in the bush, or count the catch of every canoe, list the gods of every clan, or explore the details of every ceremony, watch every birth, or sit at every death-bed, follow every artist and would-be artist as he works, and sit for hours at the feet of the only mystic or philosopher, one must always know the exact place in the whole [*of culture*] of the part that is unexplored, the probable size of the unexplored area, and, most importantly, how it fits in with those things that one is studying in detail."

The problem of the anthropologist is not that he must comprehend completely every detail to be known of a culture. Rather, he must come to know what he does not know. He must come to conceptualize and carry for quick recall the form of the cultural whole to enable him to judge the place and importance of any new or unknown part of that whole.[1]

The Attrition of Ethnocentrism as Method in Study of Culture[2]

Anthropologists undergo a wearing away of their own cultural ethnocentrism as they develop the ability to move easily in and out of culture categories known to another people. As they have learned to respond to new cues of emotion, develop appreciation for strange foods, become accustomed to alien intonations and alien concerns, anthropologists have evolved a relativistic attitude toward man and culture that is vital in their research. Cultural relativity means that any social form or act has to be understood as a part of the whole of the culture in which it occurs. The attitude of relativism is one of being liberated from the parochial truths of one culture to a freedom to be concerned with the diversity of human knowledge and experience, with all of its discords, its powerful and pervasive heterogeneity, and its dissents and divergence. The attitude of relativism is one of being freed from local orthodoxies and "eternal" verities. It is a sense of liberation from the constricting bonds of race, class, and time. The denial of the authenticity of any one culture's claim to final veracity tends to shape, direct, and color all study of culture. Cultural relativism is an attitude of mind, an awareness of self that can be imparted only to a very limited extent in the classroom, or gained from a text. It must be gained finally in the experiences of living and working for a long period in another culture. The anthropologist begins to develop his sense of cultural relativism as he reads and then travels to distant lands, experiencing in days or weeks a review of the history of technology in transportation, from jetliners moving at 500 miles per hour to wood-burning trains, to travel by mules and by foot over narrow mountain or jungle paths. In the preliminaries to his movement into a native community the anthropologist must deal with a bewildering variety of persons of different social and cultural categories, all a part of the cultural whole to be studied, from expatriate and native government officials to missionaries and traders, planters and visitors. Truths concerning native life tumble forth furiously with great assurance from the lips of these persons,

---

[1] It may be that improved and novel methods of dealing with complex cultural data through the as yet undeveloped computer technology will enable the fieldworker of the future to have a means of easily dealing with large amounts of data through a miniature, portable computer.

[2] These initial comments have been developed from a discussion by Margaret Mead (1963:603–604).

for many see themselves as experts on native origins, migrations, behavior, belief, and biological potential and limitations. When he finally arrives in the native community he is going to study, the anthropologist's senses are assaulted and often overwhelmed by a riot of new sights, sounds, and smells. Even the things he touches, from glass-hard bamboo house posts to iron so cold it burns, may be new to his experience. These sensory experiences may simultaneously please and sicken him while he struggles to adjust to living closer to the natural world than ever before in his life; his bed may be a woven grass mat laid on a bamboo floor, his latrine a clump of bushes, and his bath a tumbling, cold, mountain stream. As the anthropologist comes to have to live without the material culture so familiar in his urban Western life, while at the same time fending off, assimilating, and trying to systematically think of the sense experiences that break in waves upon him day after day, he comes to be aware of himself and his culture in new ways. He discovers how he stands, walks and gestures, the patterns and logical forms of his thoughts, his assumptions of order, progress, and time. The world about him takes on new meaning as he comes to know his informants well enough to read correctly the meaning of a hitching up of a loin cloth, or a scratching of the thumb tip across the lips.[3]

The attitude of cultural relativity has often been misinterpreted by other scholars to mean that anthropologists advocate abandonment of moral responsibility, or propose a sterile and irresponsible scientism. While cutting the hearts from sacrificial virgins has been religious ritual in one society, it clearly is homicide in others. One does not urge more permissive attitudes toward sex in a culture without recognition of the relation of such acts to other parts of culture. Anthropologists are fully aware of the limits of meaning of relativism as an attitude. They do not wear grass skirts, lip plugs, or keep five wives in American culture and then seek to justify such acts on the grounds that other cultures permit such behavior. They do not advocate infanticide or killing of the aged because other cultures, with more limited resources, have thought these acts to be ethical. Nor do most anthropologists seek to avoid responsibility for their knowledge of the scope and diversity of culture through seeking to de-emphasize or deny the role of individuals. Further, relativism should not be interpreted as meaning that anthropologists ignore the obvious unity of man as one species experiencing the similar process of birth, life, and death. A systematic search for universally valid categories of culture has been part of anthropology since the earliest period of the discipline. Anthropologists cannot escape the interdependence of cultures as they trace processes of culture history. The attitude and method of

---

[3] Writing to close friends or colleagues concerning these new experiences and keeping a journal can provide the opportunity to phrase and articulate growing self-awareness in the attrition of ethnocentrism.

relativity in the study of *one* culture has no logical extension to anthropology's ultimate concerns with *the* human species and human culture.

Some Relations between Method and Theory

In the past century systematic analyses of sets of cultural facts in their ideal relations to one another have produced an extensive body of anthropological theory. Methods of study, as orderly procedures for systematic investigation of culture, have been discussed in this text generally without reference to a body of theory. This could be misleading, for there is no question that the relationships between theory and method in cultural research, as in any discipline, are intricate and of great reciprocal influence. Methods used in deriving data shape and can alter the general principles of a theoretical statement. Theoretical statements lead to profound changes in methods of study. Many anthropologists have conceived of field methods as ways to assist them in understanding the views of natives about their behavior and lives. Malinowski (1922:4–25) has put that conviction in this form:

> These three lines of approach [*methods*] lead to the final goal, of which an Ethnographer should never lose sight. This goal is, briefly, to grasp the native's point of view, his relation to life, to realize *his* vision of *his* world.

Kluckhohn (1949:299-300) has noted: "The first responsibility of the anthropologist is to set down events as seen by the people he is studying." From methods designed to produce data on a native's view of his own culture, Linton (1936) evolved theoretical statements of considerable power, scope, and utility in recording and analyzing new culture data. Linton's concepts have made possible both more refined individual studies of culture and increasingly precise statements of a general theory of culture. The methods discussed in this text commence with the conviction of Malinowski and Kluckhohn, which is widely shared by anthropologists, that a cultural study begins through attempting to record and portray accurately the major categories of customary belief and behavior generally held by the members of a society.

But a study of culture does not end at this point. Knowing the norms of a culture provides a basis for proceeding to record whether members of a culture are conscious of their norms and the ways they use them to evade or reformulate norms in particular situations. Even this record of culture remains incomplete, for there are the objective and historical realities of culture to be accounted for in the forms of houses, designs, tools, weapons, and so on, existing through time, and in the records made by the anthropologist of a language and social action with aid of tape recorders and cameras. And a record of culture, as it consists of statements directly derived from norms, awareness of norms, and objective and historical realities, also consists of complex statements by the anthropologist concerning abstractions unknown to members of a culture, such as a bifurcate merging kinship terminology, schismogensis, prefigurative rituals, myth themes as examples of reaction formation, and so forth.[4] At each of these levels of the study of culture, the term "method" means more than specific procedures used in a field study. Methods are ways of implementing investigation of hypotheses that come from a body of theory, which, in turn, is based upon previous studies of culture. Developments of field methods for study of culture have closely followed the developments of anthropological theory, and the development of theory has very much depended on methods used. Once the contingent relationships between method and theory are clear, it becomes possible to discuss the general detail of one, or the other, without intricate cross-referencing.

The Formalization of Method

It may be useful to conclude by considering the question of whether it is really possible to formalize, or present systematically, the detail of method for the study of culture. I view this work as an effort to communicate a sense of what the anthropologist means when he talks about *methods* for the study of culture. It is likely that if the discussion had been written by another cultural anthropologist, it would have other emphases and some other material for illustration. But I am convinced that whatever their temperamental bent anthropologists must follow certain basic procedures in the field. This discussion has attempted to present only the main features of some of these methods in a form that can be read and comprehended by a reader with little acquaintance with professional anthropological literature or formal field experience. There are a variety of references listed at the close of the text which pay precise attention to the detail of particular methods for the special study of language, of social relations with relatives and with nonrelatives, of methods for the study of ritual, political, economic, and artistic behavior. The professional methods literature on each of these and other categories of culture would comprise many citations to texts, articles, sections of research reports, and monographs. The selection of readings suggested here is intended not only to extend the comprehension of methods for the study of culture, but to make it quite clear that this discussion has certain orientations resulting from my own research and experience. Readers are urged to extend this work with consideration of citations listed in the bibliography.

I believe that only someone wholly involved and fully immersed in fieldwork can really communicate the essence of cultural anthropology to

---

[4] For a discussion of and definitions of the concept of culture, see A. L. Kroeber and C. Kluckhohn (1952).

students or general readers. And since I have indicated here that research in culture involves a great deal of unique personal experience for the anthropologist, I have taken the position that it is probably unlikely there can be a rigorous, systematic, and formal presentation of methods in the study of culture like those of the natural sciences and that are overriding concerns among many sociologists, psychologists, and economists. I find this stance comfortable, for it is my conviction that so long as prime theoretical concerns in the study of culture are an attempt to record and understand the native's view of his culture and the objective and historical realities of culture, then methods for field study will have to reflect the end purpose of making a whole account of a part of the human experience. The nature of that part, if a living culture, must influence the methods used. And so full formalization of methods in the study of culture must wait until another time and for a profound change in theoretical orientations.

I would conclude by making an observation that fieldworkers must use all they know in anthropology and from related human sciences, anticipate every advance in the technology of observation, interviewing, data accumulation and analysis, and utilize it fully so that the students of two and three generations from now will have records of whole cultures from which to learn the advantages of the comparative method as a means of understanding the nature of culture. Much remains to be done in the field study of culture.

Bibliography

ADAMS, RICHARD N., and JACK J. PREISS, 1960, *Human Organization Research: Field Relations and Techniques.* Homewood, Ill.: Dorsey Press.

ADCOCK, CYRIL J., and JAMES E. RITCHIE, 1958, "Intercultural Use of Rorschach," *American Anthropologist,* 60:881–892.

————, 1959a, "Intercultural Use of Rorschach: Rejoinder to Clifton," *American Anthropologist,* 61:1090–1092.

————, 1959b, "Rejoinder to Edgerton and Polk," *American Anthropologist* 61:1093–1094.

ARCHER, WILLIAM ANDREW, 1945, "Collecting Data and Specimens for Study of Economic Plants," United States Department of Agriculture. Misc. Publ. 568:1–52.

BARRETT, S. A., 1952, *Material Aspects of Pomo Culture,* Bulletin 20. Milwaukee: Public Museum of the City of Milwaukee.

BATES, MARSTON, 1953, "Human Ecology," in *Anthropology Today,* A. L. Kroeber, ed., pp. 700–713. Chicago: University of Chicago Press.

BEALS, ALAN R., and JOHN T. HITCHCOCK, 1960 *Field Guide to India,* Field Guide Series No. 4. Washington, D.C.: National Academy of Sciences-National Research Council.

BEARDSLEY, RICHARD K., 1959, *Field Guide to Japan,* Field Guide Series No. 4. Washington, D.C.: National Academy of Sciences-National Research Council.

BATESON, GREGORY, 1941, "Experiments in Thinking about Observed Ethnological Material," *Philosophy of Science,* 8:53–68.

BATESON, GREGORY, and MARGARET MEAD, 1942, *Balinese Character: A Photographic Analysis.* New York: Special Publication of the New York Academy of Sciences, II.

BECKER, HOWARD S., and BLANCHE GEER, 1957, "Participant Observation and Interviewing: A Comparison," *Human Organization* 16:3:28–32.

BELL, J. H., 1953, "Field Techniques in Anthropology," *Mankind,* 5:1:33–8.

————, 1955, "Observation in Anthropology," *Mankind,* 5:2:55–68.

BENNETT, JOHN W., 1948, "The Study of Cultures: A Survey of Technique and Methodology in Field Work," *American Sociological Review*, 13:672–689.

BENNETT, W. C., 1949, "Habitations," in *Handbook of South American Indians*, Julian Steward, ed., Vol. 5:1–20. Washington, D.C.: Smithsonian Institution, Bureau of American Ethnology.

BIRDWHISTELL, RAY L., 1952, *Introduction to Kinesics; an Annotation System for Analysis of Body Motion and Gesture*. Louisville, Ky.: The University of Louisville.

BLACK, M., 1957, *New Key to Weaving*. Milwaukee: Bruce.

BLOCH, BERNARD, and GEORGE L. TRAGER, 1942, *Outline of Linguistic Analysis*. Baltimore Linguistic Society of America, Waverly Press.

BLOOMFIELD, LEONARD, 1942, *Outline Guide for the Practical Study of Foreign Languages*. Baltimore Linguistic Society of America, Waverly Press.

BLUM, FRED H., 1952, "Getting Individuals To Give Information to the Outsider," *Journal of Social Issues*, 8:3:35–42.

BOAS, FRANZ, 1920, "The Methods of Ethnology," *American Anthropologist*, 22:311–321.

BRITISH ASSOCIATION FOR THE ADVANCEMENT OF SCIENCE, 1852, *A Manual of Ethnological Inquiry; Being a Series of Questions Concerning the Human Race, Prepared by a Subcommittee of the British Association for the Advancement of Science Appointed in 1851 and Adapted for the Use of Travellers and Others in Studying the Varieties of Man*. London: Taylor and Francis.

BRITISH MUSEUM (NATURAL HISTORY)
Instructions for collectors:
No. 2 *Birds and Their Eggs*, 9th ed., 1954;
No. 3 *Reptiles, Amphibians and Fishes*, 6th ed., 1953;
No. 4A *Insects*, 3d ed., compiled by John Smart, rev. by. W. E. China, 1954;
No. 9A *Invertebrate Animals Other Than Insects*, 2d ed., 1954;
No. 10 *Plants*, 6th ed., 1957;
No. 11 *Fossils, Minerals and Rocks*, 6th ed., 1956;
No. 12. *Worms*, 1932.

BUCK, P. H., 1930, *Samoan Material Culture*. Bulletin 75. Honolulu: Bernice P. Bishop Museum.

BUNZEL, RUTH, 1929, *The Pueblo Potter; A Study of Creative Imagination in Primitive Art*. New York: Columbia University Press.

CASAGRANDE, JOSEPH B., ed., 1960, *In the Company of Man: Twenty Portraits by Anthropologists*. New York: Harper & Row.

COGHLAN, H., 1954, "Metal Implements and Weapons," in *A History of Technology*, Charles Singer, ed., Vol. 1, pp. 600–662. New York: Oxford.

COLLIER, JOHN, JR. 1957, Photography in Anthropology, *American Anthropologist*, 59:843–859.

————, 1967, *Visual Anthropology: Photography as a Research Method*, New York: Holt, Rinehart and Winston, Inc.

DEAN, JOHN P., and WILLIAM FOOTE WHYTE, 1958, "How Do You Know if the Informant Is Telling the Truth?" *Human Organization,* 17:2:34–38.

DEBENHAM, FRANK, 1956, *Map Making,* 3d ed. London and Glasgow: Blackie.

DENSMORE, FRANCES, 1936, *The American Indians and Their Music.* New York: The Woman's Press.

DOLLARD, JOHN, 1935, *Criteria for the Life History.* New Haven, Conn.: Yale University Press.

EVANS, I. H. N., 1922, *Among Primitive Peoples in Borneo.* London: Seeley, Service and Company.

————, 1953, *The Religion of the Tempasuk Dusuns of North Borneo.* New York: Cambridge University Press.

EVANS-PRITCHARD, E. E., 1952, *Social Anthropology.* New York: Free Press.

FIRTH, RAYMOND, ed., 1957, *Man and Culture: An Evaluation of the Work of Bronislaw Malinowski.* New York: Humanities Press.

FORTUNE, REO F., 1935, *Manus Religion.* Philadelphia: American Philosophical Society.

FOSBERG, FRANCIS R., 1960, "Plant Collecting as an Anthropological Field Method," *El Palacio,* 67:4:125–139.

FRAZER, SIR JAMES G., 1916, *Questions on the Customs, Beliefs, and Langauges of Savages,* 3d ed. London: Cambridge University Press.

GALLAHER, ART., 1961, *Plainville Fifteen Years Later.* New York: Columbia University Press.

GLEASON, HENRY A., JR., 1955, *An Introduction to Descriptive Linguistics.* New York: Holt, Rinehart and Winston, Inc.

GOODENOUGH, WARD H., 1956, "Componential Analysis and the Study of Meaning," *Language,* 32:195–216.

GREAT BRITAIN METEOROLOGICAL OFFICE, 1956, *Observer's Handbook.* London: Her Majesty's Stationery Office.

GUDSCHINSKY, SARAH C., 1967, *How To Learn an Unwritten Language.* New York: Holt, Rinehart and Winston, Inc.

HADDON, A. C., and J. HORNELL, 1936–1938, *Canoes of Oceania,* 3 vols. Special Publications, 27, 28, 29. Honolulu: Bernice P. Bishop Museum.

HALLOWELL, A. IRVING, 1956, "Psychological Leads for Ethnological Field Workers," in *Personal Character and Cultural Milieu,* Douglas G. Haring, ed., 3d rev. ed., pp. 341–388. Syracuse, N.Y.: Syracuse University Press.

HAUSER, PHILIP M., and OTIS DUDLEY DUNCAN, ed., 1959, *The Study of Population: An Inventory and Appraisal.* Chicago: University of Chicago Press.

HEINE-GELDERN R., ed., 1958, *Bulletin of the International Committee on Urgent Anthropological and Ethnological Research,* Number 1. Vienna: Committee's Secretariat.

HENRY JULES, and MELFORD E. SPIRO, 1953, "Psychological Techniques: Projective Tests in Field Work," in *Anthropology Today,* A. L. Kroeber, ed., pp. 417–429, Chicago: University of Chicago Press.

HENRY, JULES, and others, 1955, "Symposium: Projective Testing in Ethnography," *American Anthropologist,* 57:245–270.

HERSKOVITS, M., 1954, "Some Problems of Method in Ethnography," in *Method and Perspective in Anthropology,* Robert F. Spencer, ed., pp. 3–24. Minneapolis: University of Minnesota Press.

HILGER, SISTER M. INEZ, 1960, *Field Guide to the Ethnological Study of Child Life,* Behavior Science Field Guides, Vol. 1. New Haven, Conn.: Human Relations Area Files Press.

HOCKETT, CHARLES F., 1958, *A Course in Modern Linguistics.* New York: Macmillan.

HOLMBERG, ALLAN R., 1955, "Participant Intervention in the Field," *Human Organization,* 14:1:23–26.

HONIGMANN, J. I., 1955, "Sampling Reliability in Ethnological Field Work," *Southwestern Journal of Anthropology,* 11:282–287.

HUTCHINSON, H. W., 1960. *Field Guide to Brazil,* Field Guide Series No. 5. Washington, D.C.: National Academy of Sciences–National Research Council.

HYMES, DELL H., 1959, "Bibliography: Field Work in Linguistics and Anthropology," in *Studies in Linguistics,* 14:82–91. Department of Anthropology and Linguistics, University of Buffalo.

KARPELES, M. ed., 1958, *The Collecting of Folk Music and Other Ethnomusicological Material: A Manual for Field Workers.* London: International Folk Music Council and Royal Anthropological Institute of Great Britain and Ireland.

KEESING, FELIX M., 1959, *Field Guide to Oceania.* Field Guide Series No. 1. Washington, D.C.: National Academy of Sciences-National Research Council.

KLUCKHOHN, CLYDE, 1938, "Participation in Ceremonials in a Navaho Community," *American Anthropologist,* 40:359–369.

———, 1949, *Mirror for Man.* New York: McGraw-Hill.

———, 1951, "The Study of Culture," in *The Policy Sciences: Recent Developments in Scope and Method,* D. Lerner and H. Lasswell, eds., pp. 86–101. Stanford, Calif.: Stanford University Press.

KROEBER, A. L., 1939, *Cultural and Natural Areas of Native North America.* Berkeley and Los Angeles: University of California Press.

———, 1957, "Ethnographic Interpretation," 1–6. *University of California Publications in American Archaeology and Ethnology,* 47:2:191–234.

———, and C. KLUCKHOHN, 1952, *Culture: A Critical Review of Concepts and Definitions.* Cambridge, Mass.: Papers of the Peabody Museum of American Archaeology and Ethnology, Harvard University, Vol. 48.

KURATH, GERTRUDE P., 1960, "Panorama of Dance Ethnology," *Current Anthropology,* 1:233–254.

LAHEE, F. H., 1961, *Field Geology,* 6th ed. New York: McGraw-Hill.

LEWIS, OSCAR, 1953, "Controls and Experiments in Field Work," in *Anthropology Today,* A. L. Kroeber, ed., pp. 452–475. Chicago: University of Chicago Press.

LINTON, R., 1936, *The Study of Man*. New York: Appleton.

LOUNSBURY, FLOYD G., 1953, "Field Methods and Techniques in Linguistics," in *Anthropology Today*, A. L. Kroeber, ed., pp. 401–416. Chicago: University of Chicago Press.

LOWIE, ROBERT H., 1953, "Ethnography, Cultural and Social Anthropology," *American Anthropologist*, 55:527–34.

MALINOWSKI, BRONISLAW, 1922, *Argonauts of the Western Pacific*. London: Routledge (1961. New York: Dutton.)

———, 1935, *Coral Gardens and Their Magic*, 2 vols. London: G. Allen.

MEAD, MARGARET, 1931, "The Primitive Child," in *Handbook of Child Psychology*, Carl Murchison, ed., pp. 669–687. Worcester, Mass.: Clark University Press.

———, 1933, "More Comprehensive Field Methods," *American Anthropologist* 35:1–15.

———, 1939, "Native Languages as Field-Work Tools," *American Anthropologist*, 41:189–205.

———, 1946, "Research on Primitive Children, in *Manual of Child Psychology*, Leonard Carmichael, ed., pp. 667–706. New York: Wiley. Second ed., 1954, pp. 735–780.

———, 1949, "How an Anthropologist Writes," in *Male and Female*, pp. 22–47. New York: Morrow.

———, 1951, Appendix 1: "Practical and Theoretical Steps Involved in This Research," in *Growth and Culture, a Photographic Study of Balinese Childhood*, by Margaret Mead and Frances C. Macgregor, pp. 189–208. New York: Putnam.

———, 1956*a*, "Some Uses of Still Photography in Culture and Personality Studies," in *Personal Character and Cultural Milieu*, Douglas Haring, ed., 3d rev. ed., pp. 79–105. Syracuse, N.Y.: Syracuse University Press.

———, 1956*b*, "Methods Used in This Study," (Appendix I) in *New Lives for Old*, pp. 481–501. New York: Morrow.

———, 1959*a*, *An Anthropologist at Work: Writings of Ruth Benedict*. Boston: Houghton Mifflin.

———, 1959*b*, *People and Places*. Cleveland and New York: World Publishing.

———, 1959*c*, "Apprenticeship under Boas," in *The Anthropology of Franz Boas*, Walter Goldschmidt, ed., pp. 29–45. San Francisco: Howard Chandler.

———, 1963, "Anthropology and an Education for the Future," in *The Teaching of Anthropology*, D. Mandelbaum, G. W. Lasker, and E. M. Albert, eds., American Anthropological Association, Memoir 94:595–607.

MERTON, ROBERT K., MARJORIE FISKE, and PATRICIA L. KENDALL, 1956, *The Focused Interview: A Manual of Problems and Procedures*. New York: Free Press.

MILLAR, C. E., L. M. TURK, and H. D. FOTH, 1958, *Fundamentals of Soil Science*. New York: Wiley.

MONTAGU, M. F. A., 1960, *A Handbook of Anthropometry*. Springfield, Ill.: Thomas.

MURDOCK, GEORGE P., *et al*, 1960, *Outline of Cultural Materials*, 4th rev. ed. Behavior Science Outlines, Vol. 1. New Haven, Conn.: Human Relations Area Files, Inc.

NETTL, BRUNO, 1954, "Recording Primitive and Folk Music in the Field," *American Anthropologist*, 56:1101–1102.

NEWMAN, PHILIP L., 1965, *Knowing The Gururumba*. New York: Holt, Rinehart and Winston, Inc.

NIDA, EUGENE, 1945, "Linguistics and Ethnology in Translation Problems," *Word*, 1:194–208.

———, 1947, "Field Techniques in Descriptive Linguistics," *International Journal of Anthropological Linguistics*, 13:138–46.

———, 1950, *Learning a Foreign Language: A Handbook for Missionaries*. New York: Committee on Missionary Personnel, Division of Foreign Missions, National Council of the Churches of Christ in the U. S. A.

———, 1957, *Morphology: The Descriptive Analysis of Words*, 2d ed., Ann Arbor, Mich.: University of Michigan Publications—Linguistics.

PAUL, BENJAMIN D., 1953, "Interview Techniques and Field Relationships," in *Anthropology Today*, A. L. Kroeber, ed., pp. 430–451. Chicago: University of Chicago Press.

PICKETT, A. G., and M. M. LEMCOE, 1959, *Preservation and Storage of Sound Recordings*. Library of Congress, Superintendent of Documents. Washington, D.C.: U. S. Government Printing Office.

PIDDINGTON, RALPH, 1957, *An Introduction to Social Anthropology*, Vol. 2. Edinburgh: Oliver and Boyd.

PIKE, KENNETH L., 1947, "How to Learn a Language," in *Phonemics: A Technique for Reducing Languages to Writing*, pp. 228–31. University of Michigan Publications in Linguistics, Vol. 3. Ann Arbor, Mich.: University of Michigan Press.

POWDERMAKER, HORTENSE, 1966, *Stranger and Friend: The Way of an Anthropologist*. New York: Norton.

RADCLIFFE-BROWN, A. R., 1913, "Three Tribes of Western Australia," *Journal of the Royal Anthropological Institute*, 43:150–151.

———, 1958, "The Methods of Ethnology and Social Anthropology," in *Method in Social Anthropology; Selected Essays by A. R. Radcliffe-Brown*, M. N. Srivinas, ed., pp. 3–38. Chicago: University of Chicago Press.

RADIN, PAUL, 1933, *The Method and Theory of Ethnology: An Essay in Criticism*. New York: McGraw-Hill.

RAY, VERNE, 1952, "Techniques and Problems in the Study of Human Color Perception," *Southwestern Journal of Anthropology*, 8:251–59.

REDFIELD, R., 1953, *The Primitive World and Its Transformations*. Ithaca, N.Y.: Great Seal Books.

REICHARD, G. A., 1936, *Navaho Shepherd and Weaver*. New York: Augustin.

RICHARDS, AUDREY I., 1939, "The Development of Field Work Methods in Social Anthropology," in *The Study of Society,* F. C. Bartlett, M. Ginsberg, E. J. Lindgren, and R. H. Thouless, eds., pp. 272–316. London: Routledge.

RICHARDSON, STEPHEN, 1960, "A Framework for Reporting Field-Relations Experiences," in *Human Organization Research,* Richard N. Adams and Jack J. Preiss, eds., pp. 124–139. Homewood, Ill.: Dorsey Press.

ROMNEY, A. K., n. d., *Social Structure: The Collection and Interpretation of Data,* in press. New York: Holt, Rinehart and Winston, Inc.

ROWE, JOHN H., 1953, "Technical Aids in Anthropology: A Historical Survey," in *Anthropology Today,* A. L. Kroeber, ed., pp. 895–940. Chicago: University of Chicago Press.

ROYAL ANTHROPOLOGICAL INSTITUTE OF GREAT BRITAIN AND IRELAND, 1951. *Notes and Queries on Anthropology,* 6th ed. London: Routledge. (Earlier editions: 1874; 1892; 1899; 1912; 1929.)

RUTTER, O., 1929, *The Pagans of North Borneo.* London: Hutchinson.

SCHUSKY, E., 1965, *Manual for Kinship Analysis.* New York: Holt, Rinehart and Winston, Inc.

SHEPARD, A. O., 1956, *Ceramics for the Archaeologist.* Washington, D.C.: Carnegie Institution of Washington Publication 609.

SPENCER, ROBERT F., ed., 1954, *Method and Perspective in Anthropology. Papers in honor of Wilson D. Wallis.* Minneapolis: University of Minnesota Press.

SPINDLER, GEORGE, 1955, "Projective Testing in Ethnography," *American Anthropologist,* 57:259–262. (See Henry, J., and others, 1955).

STURTEVANT, WILLIAM C., 1959, A Technique for Ethnographic Note-Taking, *American Anthropologist,* 61:677–678.

THOMAS, WILLIAM L., JR., ed., 1956, *Man's Role in Changing the Face of the Earth.* Chicago: University of Chicago Press.

TYLOR, E. B., 1906, "Anthropology" in *Hints to Travellers,* 9th ed., pp. 106–129. London: Royal Geographical Society.

VOEGLIN, C. L., and ZELLIG S. HARRIS, 1945, "Linguistics in Ethnology," *Southwestern Journal of Anthropology,* 1:455–465.

WHYTE, WILLIAM FOOTE, 1960, "Interviewing in Field Research," in *Human Organization Research,* Richard N. Adams, and Jack J. Preiss, eds., pp. 352–374. Homewood, Ill.: Dorsey Press.

WILLIAMS, THOMAS R., 1960, "A Survey of Native Peoples of North Borneo," *Sociologus,* 10:170–174.

———, 1961*a,* "A Tambunan Dusun Origin Myth, *Journal of American Folklore,* 74:68–78.

———, 1961*b,* "Ethnohistorical Relationships and Patterns of Customary Behavior Among North Borneo Native Peoples," *Sociologus,* 11:51–63.

———, 1962*a,* "Form, Function and Culture History of a Borneo Musical Instrument, *Oceania,* 31:178–185.

———, 1962*b,* "Archaeological Research in North Borneo," *Asian Perspectives, The Bulletin of the Far-Eastern Prehistory Association,* 6:230–231.

————, 1962c, "Tambunan Dusun Social Structure," *Sociologus*, 12:141–157.

————, 1963a, "The Form and Functions of Tambunan Dusun Riddles," *Journal of American Folklore*, 76:95–110; 141–181.

————, 1963b, "The Form of a North Borneo Nativistic Behavior," *American Anthropologist*, 65:543–551.

————, 1965, *The Dusun: A North Borneo Society*. New York: Holt, Rinehart and Winston, Inc.

————, 1966, "Cultural Structuring of Tactile Experience in a Borneo Society," *American Anthropologist*, 68:27–39.

WOLFE, ALVIN W., 1959, *Field Guide to West and Central Africa*. Field Guide Series No. 2, Washington, D.C.: National Academy of Sciences-National Research Council.

Recommended Reading

Ethnographies to Illustrate
Field Methods in Study of Culture

These descriptions and analyses of culture and social life demonstrate the broad range of field methods and theory used in cultural anthropology. Each work is considered a model of a particular type of field research.

ARENSBERG, CONRAD M., and SOLON T. KIMBALL, 1940, *Family and Community In Ireland*. Cambridge, Mass.: Harvard University Press.
    An account of culture and society in rural farming villages in Ireland.
LEACH, EDMUND R., 1961, *Pul Eliya, a Village in Ceylon: A Study of Land Tenure and Kinship*. Cambridge: Cambridge University Press.
    A study of the social life and economics of a rural farming community in Ceylon, following field methods commonly used by British anthropologists.
LEWIS, OSCAR, 1959, *Five Families: Mexican Case Studies in the Culture of Poverty*. New York: Basic Books.
————, 1961, *The Children of Sanchez: Autobiography of a Mexican Family*. New York: Random.
Innovative studies of family life in a Mexican setting of low incomes and cultural deprivation.
MEAD, MARGARET, 1938, *The Mountain Arapesh:* (I), "An Importing Culture," *Anthropological Papers of The American Museum of Natural History,* Vol. 36, Pt. 3, 1938. pp. 145–349.
————, 1940 (II), "Supernaturalism" idem, Vol. 37, Pt. 3, 1940. pp. 317–451.
————, 1947 (III), "Socio-Economic Life"; idem. Vol. 40, Pt. 3, 1947 pp. 163–479.

————, 1947 (IV), "Diary of Events in Alitoa" idem, Vol. 40, Pt. 3, 1947, pp. 163–419.

————, 1949 (V), "The Record of Unabelin with Rorschach Analyses" idem, Vol. 41, Pt. 3, 1949, pp. 289–390.

This study of an isolated, nonliterate New Guinea people is the model for systematic study and analysis of culture and social life in such settings.

SPICER, EDWARD, 1940, *Pascua: A Yaqui Village in Arizona.* Chicago: University of Chicago Press.

A study of social life and culture of a displaced Mexican Indian community employing adaptations of British anthropological field methods to American anthropological concerns.

WEST, JAMES, 1945, *Plainville, U. S. A.* New York: Columbia University Press.

An account of culture and society in a contemporary American small town, which is considered a prototype for such studies.